MEZCAL

ALSO BY CHARLES BOWDEN

Killing the Hidden Waters (1977)
Street Signs Chicago: Neighborhood and Other Illusions of Big-City Life, with Lewis
    Kreinberg and Richard Younker (1981)
Blue Desert (1986)
Frog Mountain Blues, with Jack W. Dykinga (1987)
Trust Me: Charles Keating and the Missing Billions, with Michael Binstein (1988)
Red Line (1989)
Desierto: Memories of the Future (1991)
The Sonoran Desert, with Jack W. Dykinga (1992)
The Secret Forest, with Jack W. Dykinga and Paul S. Martin (1993)
Blood Orchid: An Unnatural History of America (1995)
Chihuahua: Pictures From the Edge, with Virgil Hancock (1996)
Stone Canyons of the Colorado Plateau, with Jack W. Dykinga (1996)
Juárez: The Laboratory of our Future, with Noam Chomsky, Eduardo Galeano, and
    Julián Cardona (1998)
Eugene Richards, with Eugene Richards (2001)
Down by the River: Drugs, Money, Murder, and Family (2002)
Blues for Cannibals: The Notes from Underground (2002)
A Shadow in the City: Confessions of an Undercover Drug Warrior (2005)
Inferno, with Michael P. Berman (2006)
Exodus/Éxodo, with Julián Cardona (2008)
Some of the Dead Are Still Breathing: Living in the Future (2009)
Trinity, with Michael P. Berman (2009)
Murder City: Ciudad Juárez and the Global Economy's New Killing Fields, with Julián
    Cardona (2010)
Dreamland: The Way Out of Juárez, with Alice Leora Briggs (2010)
The Charles Bowden Reader, edited by Erin Almeranti and Mary Martha Miles (2010)
El Sicario: The Autobiography of a Mexican Assassin, with Molly Molloy (2011)
The Red Caddy: Into the Unknown with Edward Abbey (2018)
Dakotah (2019)

MEZCAL

CHARLES BOWDEN

UNIVERSITY OF TEXAS PRESS | AUSTIN

Lannan
CHARLES BOWDEN PUBLISHING PROJECT

Requests for permission to reproduce material from this work should be sent to:
Permissions
University of Texas Press
P.O. Box 7819
Austin, TX 78713-7819
utpress.utexas.edu/rp-form

♾ The paper used in this book meets the minimum requirements of ANSI/NISO
Z39.48-1992 (R1997) (Permanence of Paper).

Library of Congress Cataloging-in-Publication Data

Names: Bowden, Charles, 1945–2014, author.
Title: Mezcal / Charles Bowden.
Description: Austin : University of Texas Press, [2020] | "The first edition of Mezcal
    was published in 1988 by the University of Arizona Press."
Identifiers: LCCN 2019034592 (print) | LCCN 2019034593 (ebook)
    ISBN 978-1-4773-2024-2 (paperback)
    ISBN 978-1-4773-2025-9 (library ebook)
    ISBN 978-1-4773-2026-6 (non-library ebook)
Subjects: LCSH: Bowden, Charles, 1945–2014. | Nature—Effect of human beings on—
    Southwest, New. | Deserts—Southwest, New. | Southwest, New—Description and
    travel.
Classification: LCC F787 .B682 2020 (print) | LCC F787 (ebook) | DDC 979—dc23
LC record available at https://lccn.loc.gov/2019034592
LC ebook record available at https://lccn.loc.gov/2019034593

doi:10.7560/320242

For *Julian Hayden* and *Lawrence Clark Powell*—

two people who showed me the way to come home.

Surely I am more brutish than any man,
and have not the understanding of a man.
I neither learned wisdom,
nor have the knowledge of the holy.
Who hath ascended up into heaven, or descended?
Who hath gathered the wind in his fists?

PROVERBS 30:2-4

OPEN THE BOTTLE

I can remember the world before television. I am writing this sentence on a computer. I was born in an eighty-year-old Illinois stone house seventeen days before the atomic bomb fell on Hiroshima. The stove was wood, the toilet a privy, and carp jumped in the creek. My father planned to be buried in the front yard. He sold the ground, for a great profit, and eventually the place was leveled and made into a golf course for local executives.

I moved to the south side of Chicago at age three, escaped to the Southwest at age twelve. For my entire life I have hungered for the smell of earth and lived on carpets of cement and asphalt.

I drive fast given a good car. Speed has always been my addiction, and the velocity of things has yo-yoed me across the continent. I will never live in a stone house or believe I can be buried in the front yard.

Millions of people have lives with a similar shape, the odyssey of the generation birthed in the last great war and shipped forward into the flood tide of post-war prosperity. For us Mississippi is more than a place, the sixties is a crucible, and the panting of the earth the cry of a lover scorned and yet yearned for. We are the song of the electric guitar.

We swallowed whole the resources of the planet and accelerated to new screams of speed. And found the experience irresistible and yet wanting. Our parents were, of course, always wrong. But we are no longer children.

In my schooling, I was told about America's antiurbanism, about our pastoral dreams, about the machines in our gardens. I was told as a people we had a habit of trashing intellectuals and shrinking from the touch of modern ways. All this is well and good. I have spent my life in cities and am intoxicated by the fierceness of such places. And I have always felt something missing that led me back to empty, wild places. I have been told this is a romantic flaw in my character and the character of my countrymen. I disagree.

I think this is our character.

Sometimes I have this daydream. The Corvette is white and very fast and moves through the desert night, the asphalt singing beneath the wheels. The air is hot, the windows rolled down, rock 'n' roll roars from fine speakers. I turn the wheel and careen off into the desert. She does not even raise her voice, she is a smile, the hair carelessly blowing in the wind, the eyes staring past me into the black velvet of the night. The car bucks and dives and then lifts off and flies airborne, finally burying itself in the sand and rock. The engine dies. I revive and there is the silence of the desert night spiked by the scream of rock 'n' roll. I reach over to caress her, the lips are full. We undress and wait for a coyote dawn. This is not a nightmare. This book springs from within that idle dream.

I am almost incapable of regret. But I can reflect and think back at times. Then I drink mezcal, a cheap distillate of the agave with a worm in the bottom of the bottle. The liquor is yellow and smooth and powerful. And at the bottom, of course, is the worm, a slumbering, fleshy snippet of once living rope.

I always finish the bottle.

MEZCAL

Charles Schmid is short, silent, muscular. He bends over the hand torch in shop class. During the test in gym, he did 500 sit-ups before being interrupted by the bell for the next class. The hair is black, cut long, a dwarf Tarzan. He flunks and repeats a year of high school. I see him hanging from the rings in the gym doing the iron cross. He is the star of the team. He is the outsider in the high school world of the early sixties.

I am working at a restaurant on Broadway. Susan is a waitress, her hair a huge black beehive. She is very alive, the moves quick, the laugh a bite of energy, and I want her. Charlie comes in after midnight trailed by young girls—they look to be thirteen or fourteen. His hair is dyed an even deeper black now, makeup frames his eyes, and crushed tin cans in his boots give him a little more height. I am washing dishes and I come out front and there he is, whispering, giggling.

The farm pulls in the summer, the green pastures, the sweet smell of the cow barn. I dream of walking the fields with gun in hand, the rabbit falls in the failing light, legs flopping, and then stillness. But I do not go back.

Charlie Schmid cruises Speedway, I catch glimpses of him, sometimes he stops, we exchange fragments of sentences, he lowers his eyes, mumbles. He is a fixture. The street roars with fast cars, we drink, smoke cigarettes, flash past—I see him leaning against a truck under a light, the skin pale with makeup.

We have no drugs but we have heard of them and await their arrival in our world. The decade is about to begin.

He and some friends take a girl to a wash on the eastside, rape her, kill her, bury her. She is fifteen. Two sisters are lured from their parents' house—thirteen and fourteen I recall—and vanish. Charlie takes friends out to visit the two girls. They rest under a palo verde tree and when their dried-out bodies are pulled, they skitter across the ground with crackling sounds. Many people know of the bodies and of the killings and they are all young, high school people and no one speaks of this matter. It is early in the sixties—in twenty years such deaths and such silence will become commonplace—and this complicity is new, and exciting. The story breaks, the newspapers feed, and *Time* magazine gives Charlie a page, F. Lee Bailey flies out for the defense, takes a look, and pleads him guilty.

I can feel the power of the road. Decades are not made of years, but of cores of energy. This one will never end until the participants die and take their knowledge with them to the grave. I am lying on the floor, the television is black and white. Martin Luther King speaks before the Lincoln Memorial and says he has a dream. I am in Tucson, Arizona, the screen flickers, and the civil rights movement is a communist stunt. Barry Goldwater is bracing himself for a run at the presidency, and I know in my bones what it is to have a dream and I am ready to act out that impulse. People are locking arms on the screen. They sing "We shall overcome."

Charlie does some hard time, escapes, gets caught—he is wearing a wig near the railroad tracks in Tucson when they bag him—goes back, becomes a jailhouse poet, and is murdered in prison. I do not return to the farm for decades. There is other business. And I am not alone in this work.

Years later the vocabulary will come—speed, energy, velocity, revolution, the movement, and so on. The words will be masks for the act. When Charlie first went down, the papers were amazed that so many could know of his work, and the image that burned on the page was the crackling sound of the bodies as they were dragged across the desert ground.

The sound will remain, becoming almost a guitar chord in the new music. The amazement ceases. So does the music actually. Just the sound of the chord remains, like a word from a dead language.

The long nails gleam from very small hands and she favors colors that are dark and dripping with the songs of other eras. I notice the hands first because they speak of ambitions I do not share. When she walks down the corridors her high heels click on the linoleum and the nails flash over the swaying of her hips. The skirts are tight, always tight, the black hair coarse and sometimes cut short, sometimes long and wound into a tower.

She says, "Wanna fuck?" And then comes the laugh, a high, nervous laugh that trails off. Her arms are full of books on Latin, Shakespeare, and other sure, solid matters.

The eyes are brown, the face small, pert, cute, the button nose slightly uptilted, the mouth a bow. The dangling earrings establish a separate rhythm as she walks. Her chest is flat but the hips are rounded and swinging, a body charged with sexual signals.

I find the voice bewitching, a cooing, coaxing voice that rings clear but comes out as a whisper. That is, when she feels good about life. Sometimes the words spool from her mouth like hard wire and there is no air, no space in the solid metallic sentences. The brown eyes that usually seem so large suddenly become slits.

We are lying on a bed in a cheap motel. It is New Year's Eve and we are both twenty. The block walls shine with enamel paint, a shower curtain serves as the door to the bathroom, and the bed, an ancient metal thing, creaks. Her body glistens with sweat and the voice is a whispering instrument. Next door drunken cowboys party and drink. A voice sings out fiercely, "I don't give a damn about a green backed dollaaaar!"

She says, "Wanna fuck?" The voice is bright and childlike.

Her room is very ordered. A bookcase anchors one wall, the shelves neat with row after row of Penguin Shakespeares. No other author is permitted. The portable stereo plays Josh White—perhaps "Empty Bed Blues" or "Jelly, Jelly"—she has all his albums. It is 1966 and this is not a fashionable choice. She is very fond of antique tastes. She is very conscious of style. I swallow a glass of Jack Daniels. I cannot afford such good stuff but I am drinking it out of quart bottles anyway to please her.

She favors drugs—pills, marijuana, acid, uppers, downers, anything—just make sure it is drugs. She will toss down a drink but it is not the same. Her lips leave a bright red imprint on the filter of her cigarette. The blues chords ring from the cheap stereo.

We are in a garage on a bed. A single bare bulb dangles from the ceiling. On the floor a tower of magazines: nudist publications, soft-core pornography, hard-core pornography, overexposed, poorly framed shots of lips, crotches, breasts, cocks, asses, legs, arms, hands and now and then a face. Dylan is playing. She does not approve. She wants blues.

The war flashes toward incandescence in Asia, the crowds are beginning to form in the streets (we see them on television). Everything seems to be happening faster and faster. We are in a Mexican restaurant in Tucson, the floors cold red tile, the walls burnt adobe. She smiles like a child and proudly raps her long nails on the pile of typescript. She begins to read and I listen politely and at first inattentively. I slowly recognize the form—she is rewriting *Romeo and Juliet.* The big eyes sparkle, the pert mouth beams with pleasure, the voice reads with pleasure.

Romeo has butt-fucked Juliet and now she is going down on him. He reaches and pinches her nipples very hard. The voice crackles with energy. A middle-aged Mexican waitress arrives with salsa, chips, two beers. The voice makes no pause, the waitress hesitates, then the words register. The food and beverages are slammed down, the feet quickly retreat across the serene red floor. Noticing none of this, she continues to read out loud for hours. The words bounce off the tiles like shiny, new coins.

The car stops on a winter night. She slips off her clothes—the plastic seat covers are ice under our warm flesh.

There is a call. She is at a motel. A middle-aged man wearing boxer shorts sits on the bed. He quickly dresses and leaves. She is in panties and a tiny bra. These things happen. She vanishes from time to time and then there is a call. She reappears.

That is Susan.

HE HAS CROSSED some Mexican guys in junior high and now he must pay. He is thin, the face an angular jumble of bones. He has the look of a wolf. The languages come easily—English, Spanish, some Yaqui—but the words come slowly and slouch from his mouth with sideways glances, pausing and sniffing the air before they reveal themselves. The smile is frequent, the eyes often hard crystals of pain.

He will face his foes on the way home. We sit across from each other at hard, wooden desks. He has a sap, two boot knives, plus a switchblade. Then the bell rings, school is over and he runs the gauntlet. The next I hear he is spending a year in a Texas military academy.

Nothing changes as the years pile up on him. His adventures sharpen the image and the stance and finally the mask becomes the identity. He is always first—the first to wreck a car, to get good bottles of whiskey, roll a joint, drop some acid. Taste some smack. The first to flunk out of college. He gets to the Amazon basin by hook or crook, and makes, barters, begs—somehow gets a dugout and paddles down the river to the sea. The first.

He has an idea. We will drive to Oaxaca, buy some of the renowned machetes produced there, and then, hunt *el tigre*. Susan will come along. He is very convincing. I cannot resist. We are all young and the empire has become very dull and safe. We are ready for stronger fare. It is time, past time.

Susan puts her tongue in my mouth, the nails rake my back, the body tense yet sensual. The masks fall. She cannot say these things, none of us can. But the feeling is there, an underground river looking for the light of day. We have our beliefs, not on a list, but in our bodies, long agendas of things to taste, to do. To escape. My fingers brush against her bare skin, and the phonograph plays on. There is no future in the bed, but if only we could get up, get dressed, pack.

Jake lines up a good machine.

He sells the idea very well.

That is Jake.

THE JEEP IS crammed with packs, clothes, marijuana, pills, mountains of junk. We crowd in the front seat, Susan sitting regally in the center. My body reeks of fatigue. I am a few weeks shy of my twenty-first birthday and I have just completed my bachelor's degree in two years and ten months. This fact is very important to me.

I have prepared for this trip simply. I have purchased a new pair of Levi's, fattened my six-foot-four-inch frame to 185 pounds, and packed two volumes of Perry Miller's *The New England Mind*. I suck down a joint and wait for the bliss. This is a good moment for me. I have not touched drugs for the two years and ten months of my schooling. Now the discipline cracks, and I smile at the brittle pieces of my former regimen clattering on the floor of the jeep. I put my arm around Susan and inhale deeply.

At the border, the Mexican customs guys swarm the machine. They peer inside and poke around a bit and then look expectantly: the bite. A couple of bucks or they will empty the whole load and spread everything out on the highway for the wind to blow away.

We do not want this to happen. Besides the dope, we've got guns we hope to sell in central Mexico. Jake has heard reports of right-wing landowners careening around in trucks with mounted machine guns and chrome sidearms on their fat hips. We have brought our wares for this market. There is stereo equipment also and other appliances barred by Mexico's high tariff wall. We are a little drunk and our bellies are stuffed with Kentucky Fried Chicken. It is, of course, 1966 and if you are young everything is either a lark or a war.

The mood is calm, the customs agents amiable predators in their dirty green slacks, polished belts. Jake jabbers merrily with the officials. Susan hikes her skirt up high on one hip; she wears no underwear. The customs men lose their concentration and grow sloppy in their search.

Jake smiles and eyes the Mexicans with amusement. He reaches into his pocket for the money, jerks his hand out and a .357 Magnum cartridge rolls across the pavement.

I step on it. No one says a word. He reaches deeper into his pocket. This one takes real money.

WE ARE ALWAYS loaded. The land and faces blur past. Oak trees and grass, a high river valley, then the road slips down and hits creosote desert. A huge jar of pills rests on the seat, all those colors and shapes, and we swallow fistfuls. Jake drives very badly or very well. It depends upon your point of view. The tires scream on the curves, he blindly passes huge trucks, and steers fly past the windshield as he needles through herds at 70 mph.

The sea meets us at Guaymas. We eat in a cafe, French doors open onto the street. I stare at the tops of people's heads and swallow shrimp. Susan is all bright smiles, little girl laughs. We are her valets, her drivers, and she is on tour. Nearby the cathedral is empty of worship. The stained-glass windows peek from behind protective wire mesh. Susan chain smokes and smiles at herself.

We head a few miles north of town, turn, and spread our blankets on the beach next to the Miramar Hotel. The water is flat as glass, the sands empty, the hotel a relic from earlier decades. I drink in the bar amid bamboo and South Sea echoes. It is a holiday and people begin to arrive and stake out the beach. Soon there are soldiers in the bar, young, brown-faced men with Indian features and hard hands. They hold their rifles at the ready. Mexico prepares to indulge. The July air moves across our skin; it is very soft and sensuous. The ocean broods before us and at our backs thousands of square miles of desert wait with thorned trees and saguaros. I smell the salt.

We sleep on the beach curled up under blankets. Music drifts through the blackness, voices rise with song. I sip from a bottle of Club 45 brandy, very cheap and warm. Susan sucks on a joint. There is no conversation. Small rounded stones dot the sand and I toss all night. We do not go into the water. We swallow pills.

Mountains cradle the small bay, dabs of islands blaze white with bird shit. The waves are small and go lap, lap, lap. The bay arcs out toward a headland. I first visited that point when I was fourteen. We rumbled down a dirt road, the truck rocking in the ruts, my father peering through his bifocals into a brilliant sunset. Indians huddled under ramadas, their small open fishing boats beached before them. They had bad teeth. The old man rolled his limp cigarettes, the pelicans fed, and sand sharks moved through the shallows. We stayed a day or two and marveled. I made notes in a blue school ledger and my father read. He was drawn to the Indians. We cooked outside, they visited and inspected, we were neighbors. I was not quite at ease.

Screams of gulls knife in from the bay. I brush my hand against Susan's body, the nipples are hard. The waves lap and soothe the entire beach. Along the arc of the bay, the Indians are gone, condos are erupting and a resort belt called the Sonoran coast is booming. Soon a movie called *Catch-22* will be filmed here and years after that, the set where ancient bombers played becomes the site of a Club Med with fine-looking women parading barebreasted.

I never see it coming.

My hand brushes the coverlet and it is cool, flows down Susan's body and it is warm. We drink brandy, trade-off tokes on joints. I have just graduated and feel very little. The last few months I choked on scholarship interviews in hotel suites with committees of sad adults. They would ask questions and then make notes and send them off to yet more committees that award fellowships, various forms of dole. What do you think of Count Rumford's work? Sketch the history of natural law, please.

Breakfast in the hotel bar is a straight shot. We brush our teeth in the bathroom. The soldiers watch with blank Indian faces, hands still on their rifles, hooded eyes on Susan's ass. The barkeep washes last night's glasses and as he stacks them they clink. Out the door, birds sing in the trees.

I swallow a double amphetamine.

We go south, make a brief stop at Empalme and chew raw shrimp with a squeeze of lime. On the tidal flats, we find the brothel and a fat whore sits on a car hood proud in her skin-tight Levi's. She glares at us with contempt.

Susan talks of her lover who is built like a Greek god. She is a very small person, but he is very large, very hard, and bold. He is my lover, she purrs. She looks like an elf as she recounts his exploits of ardor and skill. He likes to take her clothes off and then tie her up and whip her. She smacks her lips as she says this and her voice grows with excitement. The feel of the rope on her wrists and ankles, the lashings, his hard muscles. He never speaks in her account … he acts. He is married and has a child, she continues. The wife is contemptible, a human nothing. Her lover's father is a minister. Her lover, she beams, is very fucked up. Jake and I ask no questions. This is not a conversation.

The 4 × 4 is hardly a week old and Jake pushes and pushes it. With less than a thousand miles on the engine, he wants to probe deep into its heart. We leave the road somewhere, the scent of the ocean drifts across the mesquite. The machine lurches down a dirt track, the long branches of the trees scratching fine lines into the bright paint. We light a joint. Suddenly we come upon a lean-to in the brush. No one is home. A couple of pallets lie on the ground, pots and pans hang from limbs. I feel I have walked through a bedroom door. Then the trees give way and sunlight bounces off the hood and the jeep hesitates on the sand of the beach. The tide is out and the surf line tumbles a half mile ahead across a span of glistening muck.

Thousands of birds scream and wheel as they feed off the exposed flat. They are so avid for life we must turn our faces away. Jake guns the engine and we slip into this wet world. The tires spin and slide, huge globs of mud rooster tail behind us. The motor strains, the machine careens from side to side, but we keep moving forward and we accept this glide as guaranteed. Jake storms through a tidal pool, I sit staring down from my door, watching the quiet domestic habits of starfish being crushed under our weight. And then the machine stops dead.

Jake shifts from forward to reverse, the tires spin, the machine entrenches itself in the ooze. Behind us the shoreline stretches as a clean white streak with a green fringe. Ahead the sea is a frothy blue line with dabs of white. Susan stops speaking of her lover, stops speaking of anything at all. Jake grips the gear knob with a worried hand.

I get out. The ooze rises over my tennis shoes and a starfish stays silent in the muck. Small fish swirl in the little pools, crabs skitter away into holes. I pull off my shoes and enjoy the warm mud. I want to stride off into the flat and search for the perfect seashell. But I hesitate, think I must be polite, and turn and ask

Susan if she would like to take a stroll. She ignores me, stares straight ahead through the windshield and grimly sucks a joint with her red lips.

Of course when the tide returns, the vehicle will go under the waves and that will be the end of the engine. This we do not say. When I return from my tour of inspection, Jake is standing mute by the machine. Susan sits in the front seat, sucking on a cigarette now, and reading a paperback book. Gulls wheel overhead and scream with delight. She never looks up.

The tide rolls toward us, water begins to lap at the tires. I push from the back, Jake rocks through the gears, the 4 × 4 liberates itself from the suction of the mud and creeps off. We make it to the beach. When we pass the lean-to it is still empty of people and the pallets wait on the ground. At the highway, we share a joint and Jake sings a nonsense song: "Floppy-eared mule, floppy-eared mule, floppy-eared floppy-eared floppy-eared mule. Mule, Mule, Mule, Mule, Floppy-eared, floppy-eared mule."

We all join in the singing. The machine is no longer new and this seems like a very good thing to us.

We enter a city. A fat woman sits primly on a metal chair under a big mesquite tree that dominates her patio. I turn on a hose and pour water over my hot head. Jake dickers. We are in Obregón, a farm town, and she sells bootleg mezcal. She never lifts off the chair, and her black dress hangs solid as metal around her. Suddenly a gallon jug appears and we pay. The amphetamines and the mezcal form a kind of balance in our bodies and, of course, the grass weaves everything together. We do not eat that day.

Jake speaks in riddles. Susan says, "It would be interesting to put your mind into my lover's body." Words go like that, sentences whipping through the air independent of each other, thoughts that never meet another thought. And of course we have the mezcal.

We are off the road now, the 4 × 4 plunging through a thorn forest along the Rio Yaqui where the ancient towns of the tribe persist. The sky is overcast, a convincing hard plate of gray, and we sweat like beasts in the humid air. In a mile or two or three, we hit an arroyo, dive down into its expanse and are instantly stuck again. I push, Jake shifts, Susan sits serene. Nothing moves. I am splattered by mud and blobs of goo hang from my clothes. More pills.

We walk off into the thorn forest and after a mile or so stumble into a village. No one is in sight, not one living thing stirs, not a dog, a chicken, a horse, steer, goat, small child or ancient hag. Little huts lie scattered about with no apparent order. A huge adobe building, two stories high and running what seems half a city block, stands empty, roof collapsing, windows long gone, bricks melting back into the earth. I run my fingers along the rough surface and here and there detect holes punched by bullets. A Mexican garrison post, no doubt, thrown up in the endless Yaqui wars that convulsed Sonora at the turn of the century.

We do not speak. The weight of the place has cut our tongues. I can feel eyes burning into my flesh, eyes watching me everywhere, but when I turn there is no one. We begin to disappear from each other, our bodies surrender their solidness. I cannot explain this fact. Jake and Susan drift off and I go toward the big mud church. A graveyard surrounds the old walls and on each grave is a dish for food. Dead flowers lie on the soil. The graves are humps of earth and under the piles I can feel the heat of the corpses burning the soles of my feet.

I open one of the big wooden doors on the sanctuary and enter. There are no pews, the floor is hard, smooth and nothing mars its surface under the vault of the roof. The altar is almost barren—a cross and a deer head. I can still feel the eyes. The deer head is a buck and the antlers thrust up with vigor. I go back outside to the gray sky.

Little bells begin to jingle and a Mexican peddler wheels into view, his small truck alive with clanking pots, pinging cans and jars, and the ringing of those little bells. He stops, ignores me, and waits by a hut. A short brown woman emerges, makes a small purchase, and then returns to her home, the door firmly shutting behind her. I go over to the hut and stand there, minute after minute after minute. The door opens again. Two women come out with a rough wooden bench, plant it on the brown soil and motion to me. I sit. They hand me a chunk of goat cheese and disappear. I crumble the salty slab with my fingers and eat. The sky smells like rain.

After awhile, Jake and Susan come by and sit with me. We do not speak, we sense it is not permitted. Finally, we get up and walk out of the village. Our bodies are tense with speed and a light rain begins to fall like grace. We have that fierce odor that comes from amphetamine sweats and the rain mixes with this stench and softens our scent. Our clothes sag with moisture and become the angles and curves of our bodies.

We sit in the jeep, swallow mezcal and regroup. We do not believe in the possibility of success. I get out and push again, Jake flips the gears back and forth. We shovel, toss branches under the tires, think free-wheeling thoughts. The 4 × 4 will not move. We have each been stuck dozens of times and are confident in our faith that something will turn up.

A man walks out of the thorn forest. He is short, sandaled, with loose pants, open shirt, and perhaps forty years on his face. He weighs about 130 pounds and is Yaqui. The moustache is pencil thin and he moves to the back of the machine. I stand off. He begins to breathe deeply, then exhale, then breathe again. He is hyperventilating, a tactic drilled into me by coaches on my high school swim team. At last he is ready and signals Jake.

The engine strains, the gears grind in and out of forward and reverse, and then the machine surges forward and is free. I look over at the small man and see little beads of blood forming along the pores of his pencil thin moustache. I stare at his thin arms and legs and watch his drumlike chest heave. We give him the bottle of mezcal and without a sound he vanishes back into the thorn forest.

Once we regain the pavement we do not stop for food or water or rest. I am busy bouncing uppers and downers off each other and fumigating my brain with grass. Susan presses against me and I feel the warmth of her thigh, the light touch of her hair brushing my face. Her eyes smile constantly and her lips leave generous red marks on the filter of her cigarettes. I love to watch her smoke, to witness the studied way she exhales, the white stream flowing leisurely from her mouth and licking the air like a giant tongue. She looks out the window and then comes the rattling laugh.

"Mexicans," she bubbles, "are the bad part of Mexico."

And then more silence and the warmth of her body.

Hotels line the promenade along the curve of the bay at Mazatlán. We are 600 miles south of the border now. Out under the waters a statue of Christ waits for the annual blessing with wreathes by fishermen who need friends if they are to face the deep. I have been here before. Once at Eastertime I saw a fight outside a fine hotel. Two men slugged it out and sweat soaked their soft shirts as the fists thudded home. A crowd enjoyed the blows and women wearing high heels climbed atop glass tables and bounced with excitement. I remember the women the best, their faces a rich brown, the eyes alive amid smears of turquoise and black shadow. The generous hips looked lush.

We follow the bay north of town and park on the beach. The sand feels cool under our bare feet and to the south the bright lights of the city sparkle with promises. Cars pass now and then on the bay road but the engine sounds are muted by the heavy sea air. We carry blankets and make our nest by the waters, shuck our clothes, and lie under the black sky in the July heat. There is laughter and giggles, the sweet smell of grass, warm bites of brandy and the constant buzz saw of the pills ripping through our veins. Susan stretches out, her flesh assuming the shape of a small doll. She seems defenseless without her stiletto heels. Hours pass and nothing is said, just sounds, the feel of her body, the small talk of ocean slapping the shore.

I am drunk. My legs move, my body stands and marches toward the sea. The cold water swirls over my feet. My body pauses and considers, then runs toward the ocean and dives. Everything is black and cold and then the cold passes. Sinking, sinking toward the bottom, sinking into a jell of ink.

There is a slight tug, a pull, I am going. My body tumbles about, scrapes bottom, and the skin tears. Blood seeps from new wounds—I cannot see this evidence in the blackness but I am certain of the blood—and I dream of sharks cruising patiently and searching for such a clue, trim beasts snorting through the endless ocean and hoping for that part per million or per billion that fires all their cells into purpose. Then will come the ancient act. My shoulders, knees, and elbows sting with raw flesh, the pull continues and I am dragged along the coarse sea floor. I am going out with the ocean and I know it. I stay captive on the bottom. The surface does not seem possible, everything is black and tumbling and churning and now the water feels cold, very cold and the salt of the sea stings my cuts and scrapes. I swallow fear whole.

It occurs to me that I am going to die. This seems premature. I begin to fight, to thrash, to claw the fluid, my hands grabbing water to take me to the land. But these efforts do not matter. The pull of the sea continues and I slide and scrape toward deeper, blacker places. Suddenly I bob to the surface, a reject of the ocean, and I eat the air like meat, chewing delicious mouthfuls. The lights along the shore seem very far away now and I am broken by this sight. I cannot gauge the distance anymore than I can measure time. I have escaped simple units and increments. The body ignores the dispirited mind and begins to stroke toward shore against the tide. The ocean continues to pull toward the open sea and a part of me, a large part wishes to surrender, but this desire is denied by the muscles in my limbs as they stroke and stroke and stroke.

Without warning the bottom comes up under me and I stand, walk forward out of the surf and onto the beach. My body trembles, legs and arms now leaden poles hanging limp off the torso. I fall on my knees and vomit long, wracking shudders of bile.

Stumbling along the shore, I eventually come upon Jake and Susan. They are both asleep. No one seems to know I have been gone. I light a joint and the grass calms me. The black water begins to leave my head. I relax and wonder if anything actually happened. Then I lie down and feel the sand grind against the raw flesh of my shoulders and my fingers slide in the moist blood dripping down my back.

I study the outline of Susan's face in the darkness and the peaceful contours of her cheeks in the embrace of sleep. Her hands are so very small. I must study the hands more in times of darkness when the long nails do not dominate them. Deep drags off the joint continue to help me a great deal but the chill stays in my body like an angry guest and finally I fall back and pull a blanket around me.

Dawn is much too bright and my head hurts. Men ride past on bicycles heaped with baskets and I slide clumsily into my clothes.

I speak to no one of my evening swim.

WE ARE IN a dark room and outside I hear the hum of Guadalajara traffic. The city is still beautiful. The hordes from the countryside have not yet fully arrived with their rags and expectations to set up huge shantytowns, the drug trade is polite and services visiting Yanquis who desire a discreet hit of this or that. Jake has gone somewhere to look up old friends and lovers. The phonograph plays Richard Fariña, dead that very spring from a motorcycle accident. We treasure his book, *Been Down So Long It Looks Like Up To Me*, because it makes perfect sense. I lie on the bed and listen to "Reflections On a Crystal Wind" and assume it must be about methedrine. Everything is drenched in chemicals and we all know and enjoy this fact.

The air sags with smoke from happy joints and the chenille bedspread rubs my body with bumps of fabric. Susan gets up and walks across the room to find a cigarette. I yearn for her in a way I have seldom allowed myself. This is not a matter of courtship, wooing, marriage, or sex. This is a room of blatant hunger and rich fat notes oozing from the speakers, of bright brass sketching the golden ache of beauty. Her body looks alabaster in the half light and her bare hips sway as she takes mincing steps on the cool tile floor. We do not speak ... we have not for hours. The music is sufficient, the wonderful music that makes us sometimes smile or laugh at an apt guitar chord or the squeal of a horn.

She is returning across the floor now, I hear her feet go slap slap on the cool tiles, my eyes drift across her pale skin, a white sheet of flesh, black accents of hair. She slides under the covers, the smoke swirls upward toward the ceiling, and she is warm against me. I am very grateful. Then she slides on top.

Somehow the records keep playing magically for hours, someone must be flipping the sides over and changing albums but there is simply no documentation to verify this fact. Her tongue is in my mouth and the voices wander around the room rhyming curious messages. There can be nothing better than the feel and smell and taste of Susan, the sound of the music, the dark shadows on the walls, the rough feel of the bedspread when I run my fingers across it. Susan is smiling.

I get up and pull on my Levi's and go out the door. This takes a very long time but I accomplish it. The sun is brilliant in the motel courtyard, the sky a deep blue and the leaves tropical in design and sincere in their green. White, blue, green, swirls of color. I sit in a chair and Jake is in the next chair. He has been in the city seeing about the sale of the guns or appliances or something. And I suspect he has restocked the pharmaceutical larder. I can barely hear him. He is drinking and I join in tossing down mezcal.

My head tilts back, and the colors, colors obscene in their brilliance, send me back to the farm where I was born. Skins of Holsteins, black and white swatches of hide, functioned as the rugs in the big space of the fourteen-room limestone house thrown up during the Civil War.

The flooring was oak. The creek down the hill ran green with algae, and there were chickens, turkeys, ducks, guinea hens, cattle. The garden took an acre and my mother slaughtered 200 chickens a year for the table. She cooks on a wood stove, there is always company. The privy is cold in winter. I walk through the tall grass, the blades breaking my child's stride, and the rank scent fills my nostrils. A snake whips past me and I am terrified. Crows have been sacking the orchard and an uncle has killed a blackbird from the flock and hung the corpse from an apple tree. Now the crows stay away. I hear the slap of a carp's jump, the ripples radiating out.

Jake is talking now, I look up and there are some Mexican guys, rich friends of his from the city I guess, and they are smiling from the billboard of their nice white shirts, expensive shoes and links of gold chain. I wiggle my toes in the dirt, feel the sun against my bare chest and see my mother on the back porch of the farmhouse dropping a weasel at fifty yards with one shot from a .22 rifle. My Levi's are very loose now, I must eat one of these days. One guy nods his head vigorously and smiles some more, and on his wrist a thin gold watch glows with time and money. He is very well groomed.

He walks over to our room and goes in. In a minute, he comes scurrying out and then all the Mexicans leave with quick, fleeting farewells.

I look up and Susan is standing in the doorway naked.

"When I want someone in my bed," she says, "I will put them there."

We drive down the narrow streets of the old core of Guadalajara. Jake races through blind intersections and finally we hit a Mercedes Benz. The jar of pills falls off the front seat and spills out on the floor. Jake gets out and talks, gets back in and we drive away. He has managed to strike the one Mercedes in the city that does not want to deal with the authorities either. We are charmed but of course we already knew this.

The buildings lean forward over the street and have the feel of some ancient quarter in a European city. This is the red-light district and tonight is my twenty-first birthday. I will assume my majority, vote for my leaders, partake in all the rights of my people and assume the toga of a full citizen. Susan walks beside with a tight black skirt, white blouse, and black patent leather shoes. A drop of something splats on the brilliant surface of her pumps.

"Your come," she beams.

We hire a mariachi band and it follows me. I get up from my chair in a cantina and head for the toilet. The bass, guitar, trumpet, trombone, all squeeze in with me while I piss. They play "Borracho."

We begin with beer, then explore brandy and finally assume the serious work with mezcal. Jake's eyes gleam and his face is taut with pleasure and menace. He has the look of a sly devil and mutters little gnomic fragments of speech that seem to declare that this is Mexico and Mexico is a good thing but the United States is not a good thing. The United States, he reveals, is over-specialized, over-specialized. This, one must not be.

We enter the Plaza de Mariachis, a big open space with many tables and stout wooden chairs that invite one to tilt them backwards and teeter bravely above the stone pavement. Waiters flutter about with trays of drinks and the air sparkles with music, laughter and talk. Our band still surrounds us and we sit within a horseshoe big with sound. Susan simply glows with pleasure and the mezcal struggles hopelessly against the fist of amphetamines blazing in my guts. She taps her long nails on the tabletop. Click, click, click. I delight in the crisp notes against the lush tones of the horns. I look at her shoe.

There is a stone staircase, very wide and grand, sweeping up one side of the Plaza and our table is close by this imperial gateway and Susan sits facing the steps. A dozen men or more stand on the stairway, their brown faces rippling with hope, and stare hard in our direction. Susan tilts back in her chair, her skirt hiked halfway up her thighs. I toss down a shot of mezcal and think I have never tasted anything so warm and good before. "¡Waiter, más mezcal!"

Susan whispers into my ear, "I am not wearing any panties."

The men continue to eat her with their eyes, prod each other with their elbows and wink, but choke back any gross displays of pleasure. Jake rouses himself from some deep spin of booze and grass, glances up and sees the men. He looks over at Susan almost ready to topple backward from her chair in her dedication to some instinct of sharing and his eyes tighten. The cheek bones push upward through his flesh, the outline now sharp and hard, and he stands, pulls up his shirt and there sleeps the black handle of a .357 Magnum. The air in the Plaza is so soft and warm.

The men go rigid and then magically melt away into shadows and join the darkness.

We drive all night and my stomach is sour and tight from the mezcal and other potions. Finally, the machine announces its needs and we pull over at a small gas station in a mountain village where the cold hugs the ground like an evil blanket. Jake checks the oil and then we go on. The hood flies up—we are so terrible about details of latches and locks—and smacks the windshield and it becomes a radiating sun of fine lines and cracks. We press on into the night peering through our new lens of playful refractions.

One village has a cobblestone street and as we roar past I see families huddled in one-room quarters, the glow of kerosene lanterns making their faces Rembrandt canvases. The mountain cold makes our bones want to snap.

The living room takes up most of the second floor of Jake's townhouse in Mexico City. Below the big back window, the patio has gone wild with weeds and debris. Broken concrete blocks and fragments of glass dot this rank growth. Down the street, a tiny tortilla factory hums each morning and I stand in line with the neighborhood women, actually the maids of the local residents, and wait patiently for my stack of thin, hot cakes. The tortillas fly off an old machine and the gears clatter and the chains race before my eyes. The smell reassures me about the reason for each and every day. We never eat the tortillas.

There are sights that must be seen. I climb the pyramid step by step, stand on the top under a smoggy sky and think about matters of the human heart. When I was a boy I read William

Hinckley Prescott's *The Conquest of Mexico*, the obsidian knife slashing through the chest, the filthy priests raising up the steaming heart toward god, and the pyramid does not seem enough to put a floor under such an era of dreams and great expectations. Susan sits in the 4 × 4 below and reads furiously. Smoke pours from her mouth and she remains pure in her refusal to look or examine anything preserved from the past. We drive on and visit an Englishman with a Japanese wife. He explains, "Istanbul is the next place. That is where everyone must go." Jake nods and we all appreciate our new marching orders.

The Gardens of Xochimilco are much reduced from the days of Montezuma. Mexico City has drunk the valley dry and the floating dreamland clings to a few remaining dribs and drabs. We hire a boat, and drift down the channels, the trees arching overhead. Families float past with festive faces and small barges equipped with stoves pull up and try to tempt our electric faces with piles of food. Susan grows more and more silent.

The music plays day and night and we cannot bring ourselves to sell her stereo. A tall stack of albums slowly grinds out under the aging needle and only a candle violates the purity of the room as we sprawl on the floor. Days and weeks slip by. They are one bolt of cloth, a fabric carelessly interwoven with mezcal, speed and grass, and in this rather original textile there are brief events that create tiny shudders as the powerful loom fashions the intricate pattern from the threads.

A large Mexican harp dominates the living room and Jake struggles to master the anarchy of the strings. He strums notes but stops short of melody. Susan has moments of domestic seizure. She is now standing at the kitchen sink doing dishes (who, I wonder, ever ate off them?) A clean blouse graces her shoulders, and her bare ass glows as she thunders through the art of homemaking.

There are faint moments of hesitation. I step on a scale somewhere, calculate the kilos and grams and realize that I now weigh 140 pounds. I must leave, I announce. Around midnight we all go down to the bus station. First there must be farewell drinks. Then there must be more drinks. Mezcal, naturally. Now the jeep is moving and with each turn of the wheels my head bounces against the hard metal floor. I awaken in a bed and Susan is all white flesh and her eyes are closed. A smile graces her face. I return to my duties.

The stereo begins to sound odd, the notes dragging and somewhat out of phase, the melodies slurred and repellant. Susan concludes that the current of Mexico City has tortured the delicate wires and precise calibrations of the machine's soul. She talks for hours about the difference between Mexican power and American power, her mouth snarls with AC this and DC that and her face tightens and grows red with anger. Nothing in this fucking country works, she spits, the fucking restrooms are filthy, the people are fat, ugly, and filthy. And Jake and I are no better. We are assholes, worthless assholes. She is naked and stomping around the living room in her high heels and her eyes are narrow slits.

We tie up her albums, making expert knots in the cord to secure them. The stereo is packaged like a precious infant. She is sitting there in a chair, her body prim, every hair in place, sunglasses hiding half her face, the mouth a thin line. The hands are rigid claws.

We take her to the bus station and Jake gives her a huge Prince Albert can of rolled joints and a bottle bright with pills of many colors—the vessel has the look of a candy jar full of jelly beans. She will not relent. I see the bus pull out and she refuses to look at us, her face at the window classical in its severe profile.

Jake and I now attend to the matter of the machetes, the tools of our *tigre* hunt. This takes time, perhaps a week, perhaps two weeks, I no longer have any way of knowing. There are these women from the states studying Mexican culture, that much I am sure of. We dine with them across from a funeral parlor and spend evenings listening to their sad tales of boyfriends back in Indiana. They tingle with the adventure of being in Mexico and are determined to be debauched, however briefly, before they return to their schools, families, fiancés, careers and certain fates. The women rent rooms in a fine Mexican home that has several floors and large public areas. Across the way is a park full of flowers and a maid always answers the door.

Jake is very drunk and stands in the foyer waving a pistol. There is trouble over this violation of etiquette.

I buy a first-class bus ticket and settle into my comfortable, padded seat. The air conditioner hums and purrs over my head. Suddenly there are these official-looking men in uniforms standing before me. They insist on seeing my ticket, then there is much nodding of heads. I smile but my charm has little effect. I feel very much at ease, my clothes are like old friends. I have been wearing the same shirt and trousers faithfully for five weeks. There are now hands on my arms and I am being guided from the cool womb of the fine bus. As I tumble down the steps, I catch looks of relief on the faces of the other passengers.

The gentlemen with uniforms shove me into another bus and then escort me to the very back of the machine. The seat is a slab of hardwood and there are very few people on the bus wearing shoes. An Indian woman with a baby sits down next to me but after a moment she pulls away and begins to nurse. For days I stay on that bench. I do not eat or drink or move. All my systems shut down. The other passengers bring me food, try to entice me with all manner of beverages but I will not be tricked. I will not give in. I can sense visions coming on and I wait patiently for the cleansing fire that will burn everything from my body and leave my brain a pure instrument of reason and insight.

I arrive in Nogales, Sonora, just at dusk and walk a block to the fence where the modern American customshouse awaits. There is a line and I respectfully join it. I entertain the hope that perhaps an election is going on and I will be able to taste this new delight of casting ballots and picking my representatives.

Now I hear voices and look up at men in uniforms. They speak English very well. They pull me from the line and take me to a private chamber.

"Where have you been?" they ask. "Are you an American citizen?"

They seem skeptical of my reply.

We are on the beach at Point Reyes and the surf roars. The sign says no swimming and warns of danger in the waves. She tells me her father is in the crazy place in Oklahoma. Her hair is long and her eyes intelligent—they have the fierce glare of an animal. When I picked her up a few hours ago at the apartment in San Francisco, she had scurried about finding the leather skirt, right shoes and artfully dodging the inventory of nautical hardware that clutters the small two-room place. Her roommate, who was off at work at his toils as a watchman, dreams of building a boat, a sailboat, and when he is finished crafting it, he will sail out the Golden Gate and embrace the raptures of the deep. He keeps busy stealing parts from marine supply businesses—a porthole here, a brass fitting there—against the day of his launch. But first he must deal with a bothersome heroin habit—I could do it, he laughs, I could build the ship! If only I could get off this bed!—and so the craft remains more an idea than a fact.

She has a thin body, the kind that is all bone and angles and yet somehow magically hosts breasts and curves and the chill of the fog on Point Reyes eats into her. The portable radio plays underground rock from the city; since the speakers have tasted generous dollops of sand, the sound is tinny and refreshing. Point Reyes is a natural trap, a finger of North America reaching out into the Pacific, a bony peninsula where migrating birds are tossed by storms and then confounded forever. They remain here blind to the proper avenues of escape, the right coordinates for their journeys, and, blocked from the passage of their own kind, fretting in a soup of fog, they drop out of the genetic tapestry, fail to mate, and die forgotten and literally unsung.

I have been heading here for a long time. The University of Wisconsin at Madison was polite. I sat through seminars, scribbled out an M.A. thesis and in seven months was gone—not counting earlier flights to Mexico with huge gallon jugs of sauterne (it seems always on sale) swishing on the truck seat next to me. One panic retreat became nonstop for 1600 miles, nothing but little pills to fight back sleep and, in a lonely stretch of New Mexico, giant rabbits bedeviling the driving for several hours.

Rebecca, the woman on the sand at Point Reyes, has little interest in these adventures. It is 1967 and everyone has adventures, the country brims over with madcap charges across terrain, old cars grinding up mountain passes, Benzedrine transits from coast to coast, border to border. I have put 27,000 miles on a car in eight months and feel I have been much too idle.

She wants to tell me of her life, the crazy father, the stepparents, her hungers, needs, loves, desire for more love. But I am deaf. I am a fugitive; I just do not know exactly what I flee. My last effort at school ended with me being braced against a wall by a shrink who patiently lectured me (in that adult voice children instantly loathe) about my opportunities and responsibilities, about the gratitude I should feel for my fellowship, the bright future ahead of me with solid articles in little journals, fine dinners at good tables where the hostess will speak Julia Child fluently, about the life of the mind. She told me I was sick in the head.

It was a September day and overcast—the permanent sky of the Midwest—and her office had the cool light of reason glancing off the file cabinets and comfortable chairs where clients sat and wrestled with their demons. I, alas, was not yet a client, merely a friend, but being a professional, she was willing to drop friendship like a sack of soiled laundry and give me the benefit of her knowledge. She was devoutly Catholic, and wore a sturdy tweed suit. I had two lids of grass in my loaded car outside, plus a bootjack of iron fashioned to look like a naked woman on her back with her legs spread. I had found the bootjack in an antique shop and it was my constant companion, riding soundlessly in the passenger seat.

I listened appreciatively, like a patient hearing out a dentist on the horrors of chocolate, and then, with as much grace as I could muster, lit out for the coast.

I am in a 1961 MGA, white, with a soft top. The radio is dead, well, not quite dead. The thing comes on without warning and suddenly it is two in the morning and voices start babbling. This always astonishes me. I stop in Iowa City, Iowa, for a day and finally realize I am really in the car, I have left all my goods and chattel behind me in Madison and I feel very good. In two days there will be a rock concert in San Jose, California. I do not know the bands or care. I will be there. One must have goals.

I begin to administer the pills. In Nebraska along the Platte I eat a pork chop and select a slice of apple pie from a fly-flecked glass case. That night west of Scottsbluff, the Nebraska highway patrol pulls me over at 3 A.M. The cop walks toward me with flashing lights forming brilliant coronas of color behind him. The flashlight on the face, questions of name, destination and then nothing. He just wanted to check. Okay.

Wyoming seems to slip by without memory and so does Utah—the salt flats were white and that's about it. I am sitting at the bar in a Nevada casino along the Humboldt River writing Susan a letter on a series of napkins. The text is largely song lyrics that drone on in my head. I miss her; I have carefully avoided her for six months. I sense the limits of my skills. A few months back, I was in Tucson, met a woman and rode into the foothills where we drank French wine, smoked a joint—a half pound was neatly packaged in my trunk—and made love on the hood. We descended into the city. A cop pulls me over, my top is down, the wine bottle (where is the cork!) rides between the seats. My trunk smells like a hay bale. He asks about my driving. I look up crazed and wild-eyed. He hesitates, then waves us on. These things sometimes happen. I finish the letter, a small heap of napkins lie piled up like ancient scrolls. The cocktail waitress in the casino eyes me warily. I mail it and storm off.

A barkeep in the Sierra, roused from his bed by my insistent banging on the door, looks at me with tired understanding and makes me a cup of coffee. I give him five bucks.

By the time I near Sacramento I have been awake for forty hours and my eyes have assumed a remarkable color and size. I reach San Jose just as the extravaganza begins. I park, wander the crowd, find friends—there are friends everywhere in 1967 since they are all on the road—and have a joint.

And now I am on Point Reyes in the gray fog, the sea pounding, and Rebecca, a warm goddess, by my side. I listen to her talk. She is a fine person. The radio whines and whines with its load of sand. She removes her clothing and we get warm. On the way back to the city in the fog we almost go off the cliff road. We say nothing.

I never see her again.

There is no time to stop.

The trees go gold, and red burning leaves flavor the fall air. I walk across the mall between the university library and the State Historical Society of Wisconsin. The historical society is a marble pile in the official Greco-Roman manner, a fortress thrown up during the heyday of the Populist revolt. Local lore contends its hard, grim lines spring from the fear that outraged citizens, pitchforks in hand, might storm the sacred citadels of government. The library, on the other hand, is the true child of the bleak vision that settled on the nation immediately after World War II. The sterile block of brick and facing marble would pass muster with Stalin and other recent poets of public buildings.

It is October 1969, a fine Indian summer Friday. I stroll across the mall and remember when I arrived the first time three years ago. There was a weekly vigil by silent people holding signs disputing the merits of the war in Southeast Asia. I had no interest in such matters and considered their faces examples of odd fauna. Friends would show me photographs of napalmed children and then look into my eyes for comprehension. They found none. I would continue eating, say, a slice of coffee cake. I kept to my own borders. But mainly, I vanished into San Francisco, Mexico, and other points where drugs blotted out politics.

Gradually, the demonstrations penetrated my haze. Network crews jockeyed through the crowds aiming shotgun mikes and beaming bright lights. The National Guard manned armed outposts on the roof of the historical society, their guns poking over the marble cornices. The evening air was rich with the bite of tear gas.

I begin to acclimate and try to slow down. My hair is long, I carry a standard Wisconsin beer gut, and I put in a full day's work. The wife waits at home amid books and bottles.

This fall day in 1969 I run into a friend on the mall and we talk as we amble along. Something clicks, I still do not know exactly what, and I call my wife and he calls his wife. We pile into my Volkswagen bug and drive off into the night. We are going to Washington, D.C., and we are not alone. I have stumbled into one of those moments that scholars screw up in the history books.

THE BRAKES LOCKED the first time when I took a civil service job with the state of Wisconsin to pay my bills. This, coupled with marriage, was a serious effort to park it for a while. There is a call from Susan—"I know you're married but"—and I do not yield. I must have my belief in belief. I slowly let go of dope—a little grass, but very little—and I stop the speed in November 1968. I drink beer, barrels of beer, but this is the local custom.

I am in Minneapolis and it is late afternoon. The man's body is small and shrinking, the eyes sagging with years but hard from life. His name is Vincent Dunne and in the early 1930s he shut down the Twin Cities with a general strike. The room is on the second floor and when I come up the narrow stairs, they creak. Bare walls surround an empty meeting place. The wooden floor is scarred and stained. We sit on small chairs with our hands in our laps. The big room swallows us.

Golden light pours through the south-facing window and there is no screen to prevent the yellowed curtain from hanging out and trailing against the brick wall. I study the veins on Vincent Dunne's hands, the thick fingers, the callouses. Other people are present, but I have forgotten them. Nor can I remember most of what was said. Dunne was a Trotskyist and a great organizer. He went to the federal pen under the Smith Act. Moments wallow in the rhetoric of the party line, the presenting of correct opinions as scientific hard truths, and none of this language registers. I am interested in a man, not this tape recorder, a thin man in a baggy suit, with salt-and-pepper hair cropped close, and from this sack of cheap cloth comes an iron voice.

Off to the side somewhere is a hot plate for coffee and a mimeograph machine, the survival kit of American protest. Dunne is talking of wheat fields, hop fields, lumber camps, boxcars, boxcars, boxcars, riding the rods, slipping in and out of the hobo jungles, speeches on soapboxes in the small towns, saps on the skull, eating slop in the jails. He spins a tale: he and his brothers leave Minnesota and it is the second decade of this century. Their parents stay behind and the boys hunt work. They find low wages and discover the Industrial Workers of the World. The afternoon wears on as Vincent Dunne disappears into the past. Yellow light splashes across the floor, the chairs squeak, shoes scrape, the oak floor spreads like sullen pudding.

He stares at me with a mixture of kindness and contempt, the voice keeps rolling, a low, almost soft tone, a voice telling me that I have no idea how hard it was, how rough the work was, how fierce the cops (I can feel him glaring at my long hair, my beard, my costume dress) how corrupt the judges, how rigged the whole game.

He comes back with his brothers after months of slaving in the Pacific Northwest and his mother meets them in the yard. I can smell the raw grass scent of Minnesota, the cool, green taste of the air. She stands them up, makes them strip before her and then boils their rags in a big black kettle in the yard. Then they can enter their home.

"It was terrible," he says softly, "terrible."

The moment passes, the dead language of the left returns, the adventures of the early Communist Party U.S.A., his conversion to Trotskyism, then the general strike and its tactical correctness, the work organizing truckers with over-the-road contracts, the training up of a young guy named James Hoffa, that stint in the federal pen under the Smith Act. His brother's suicide under the strain.

The talk ends. Dunne gets up and shuts the window, stacks the chairs against the wall. The sun is down and I walk out into the black summer night of Minneapolis.

I go to South Saint Paul and visit my uncle, a retired ham trimmer in the slaughterhouses, his wife a retired wiener packer. My uncle is huge, German, and drunk with the mysteries of the Masonic lodge. I tell him of my afternoon with Vincent Dunne.

He says, "Chucky, you sound just like a damn Communist."

He tries to pull me back to his America and fills my ear with reports of kin who persist out on the land. His speech is a mixture of rich English from his days studying for the Lutheran ministry and plain talk from the hard centuries of tribal blood flowing in his veins. He charges on with tales of recent visits to the family's sick and elderly, of marriages, births, lonely hours spent talking to headstones at the family burying ground, the fine smell of black Iowa soil, the exotic truths of Lutheran theology.

He drinks whiskey from a water glass and the liquor never seems to touch the flow of language or his love of life. He has always regretted that I was raised a pagan far beyond the control of tribal chieftains and is pained that I cannot say the Lord's Prayer in the mother tongue.

He is a big man and invites me to join his big country. His father once ran a still in the Depression to pay the bills, and warned my mother that come spring he might be found hanging from an apple tree if something did not happen to save the farm. This we do not speak of. My uncle has a boat and he fishes the rivers and lakes for pike. He tells me of his days with hook and line, the fight of the fish, the fine feel of the air on early morning water.

I buy a canoe, a tent, some grub and head toward a wild river in northern Wisconsin. We park by a bog, unload and push off. She is in front and this is our first real moment in the canoe. The current is dead, the water green with slime and everywhere are rotting trees, reeds, the stench of decay. Near the cattails, bubbles of gas surface from the muck below. Frogs croak and mosquitoes sing and the white craft slides out of the swamp and into the channel.

The sky goes gray, we sleep on islands, cook dinner in a cast iron frying pan, drink cheap red wine. Owls hoot. Around midnight I hear crashing sounds. I am sprawled naked in the tent, mosquitoes screaming at the netting, and then the Coleman stove flies past and smashes to the ground. Bags are ripped, pans scattered.

"Something's out there," she says.

I do not stir. The bear finishes and finally leaves. Then the raccoons come to complete the work. I crawl out into the summer night with mosquitoes needling my bare ass and I shoo away the thieves. They amble off like meatloafs.

Dew bends the grass at dawn. We see no one all day and the shore never admits to a fence, house or road. The banks lean in over the river and everything is wet, green, and blue. We slowly give up on speech and the paddles embarrass us with their small splashes. The canoe glides around a bend where two deer stand in the water drinking. We slip closer, they hear nothing, and we are ten feet away when they finally bound into the forest. Later two otters appear at the prow, dive and then swim on their backs and follow us for a half mile.

The first rapid is small. The water locks us into a route and we hit the chute by luck. She freezes at the prow and stares into the white water. We are terrified and then the craft slides into the calm below.

This continues for days and I am branded. I keep the canoe for years, the way a child insists on the security of a favored blanket. Sometimes I just go out in the garage and touch it. Then I can remember the beds of wild rice, the V of ripples off the canoe, the nights heavy like tar, the rage of the mosquitoes, the morning scum of grease in the frying pan, coffee that warms the entire world.

I am drinking with a friend in a campus bar. He is in his late thirties, going through an angry divorce, and overhead we hear helicopters as they hunt people in the night. The National Guard is everywhere and the police feel much put upon. We walk up the hill toward Bascom Hall. People race past, bright circles of searchlights follow them. The tang of tear gas floods the night air. We move through some trees and creep up to his wife's empty office. My friend picks up a big rock, pitches it through the window and the boulder comes to rest on her desktop. Revolution.

I am on State Street, the capitol glowing white a few blocks away, and people stop traffic. "Street Fighting Man" by the Stones blares from speakers in the apartment windows. A city bus is marooned, forced to turn across the lanes of traffic to be used as a barrier. The driver is red with anger. I stand near the back of the bus by the huge wheels. Two black guys push me aside, whip out big pigstickers and then I hear the whoosh of air as the tires go flat. A bartender comes out of a fraternity bar, rails against the rabble, and then goes down. A man appears from nowhere, piles into the melee and gives the barkeep a heavy boot in the small of the back.

I am building a barricade by my favorite watering hole, "The 602 Club," while across the street a supermarket burns. Cops descend. I am flat on my face on the sidewalk, my nose and cheek grinding into the cement. The plastic handcuffs cut deeply into my wrists. In the paddy wagon, the cops wave elegant little cans of mace in my face, show me their revolvers and inquire if I am a New York Jew. I realize for the first time the deep fear plaguing the authorities. I am full of beer and have to piss, but this is not permitted for hours. This game has no referees.

We are sitting in the student union cafeteria and Linda Anne, a wonderful southern lilt to her voice, worries about the population explosion, ecology, the fate of trees and small beasts. We all crush her with lectures on the vast emptiness of America, the wastefulness of capitalism, the brilliant future available in a properly managed socialist economy where the nation will be able to absorb tens of millions of additional human beings, absorb them with ease.

The canoe sleeps on a sawhorse in the garage. I sit on the floor with an open bottle of wine, reach up and touch the curve of the prow.

Everyone has had a lot to drink. A street dance has turned into a street war. We huddle in an apartment and pour whiskey against a chorus of police sirens. A friend dashes in from the vibrating streets, stands before the fireplace and talks excitedly of busts, saps on the head, clouds of gas roiling down the blocks. Then she turns and deftly vomits into the flames.

One July night, we drive to Cleveland and are put up at an empty fraternity house. I throw my bag down on the floor and am surrounded by flocks of Trotskyists holding an impromptu tent meeting. I get hungry and wander off with a guy (later, I learn he is a government snitch) into the black district which at that moment is in the throes of a window-bashing, store-torching binge. Police barricades dot the street and squads fly by with lights twirling. I enter a rib joint. The front window is gone, and the place has an open, friendly air. Everyone is black, grim and yet somehow cheerful. My order of ribs is expertly done. I stumble back to the fraternity house and have a feast on the floor. The next morning I awaken amid a small forest of empty beer cans and feel critical eyes.

We have a big meeting in an auditorium at Case-Western. Mark Rudd of the SDS Weather Bureau rails about the need to stop marching and start striking back. A squad of female body-guards stands around him, their arms locked across their chests, their faces frozen into fine scowls. Packs of federal agents pad the aisles, play-acting at being students. I am asked my politics by one and dutifully reply, "Communist, of course."

In my home, I live amid crates. The walls and ceilings are

criss-crossed with stripes of colored tape, the work of an artist who suffered a creative moment one night while drinking my booze. Frank Zappa's "Uncle Meat" snarls from the stereo. My wife is finding the married life less than perfect. I come home and she sits silent in the living room and out on the back porch a carpet of glass fragments sparkles in the sun. She has left the hammer neatly placed among the shards of broken bottles she has pulverized for hours. She offers no explanation for this pastime.

I keep the telephone on top of a sawed-off railroad tie in the corner. The machete I bought for my tiger hunt in Mexico is driven into the wood next to it. Once in a while some visitor fingers the sharp edge of the blade. They do not talk of revolution at such moments. I never meet one radical in Madison who is not appalled when he or she discovers I live in a house full of rifles, shotguns, and pistols.

In the winter nights I like to walk through the snow and feel the crunch of flakes under my boots in the twenty below air. I am a first generation college student and I look at the scholarship in my hand and shudder. I go to faculty dinners and drink and study the angry eyes of the wives. I live in the library, my hands running down the rows of books. They have every edition of Henry Miller, I am in an ark of the mind. The wind is off the frozen lake and bites at my face. This is a trap, a parking lot. A friend once told me of meeting an old rummy in a bar in Nogales, Sonora. The drunk said reality is a horse's head, a nail and dynamite. We all laughed. My boots punch hard imprints in the snow. The city is silent at such moments but the blackness promises to shatter at the touch of my gloved hand.

WE ARE CROWDED in the small green Volkswagen as we glide down the interstate in the October evening. We are excited to be moving—after all we are Americans—but hesitant about our journey. The anti-war movement has called for a national demonstration in Washington, D.C., and for me this prospect is deadly. There will be banners, a march, merciless speakers from New York and other eastern centers of zealous political thought, and thousands and thousands of smug faces. The local Madison cell of the national committee has equipped us with the address of a sound, certified liberal where we can flop in the capital.

The crops are coming in from the fields and all across the Midwest there is the feel of harvest in the night. Chicago slips by, a glowering bank of lights and dirty air, then the fury of Gary, Indiana, followed by a series of turnpike stops named after failed American poets. Huge trucks rumble along and dwarf the small car. It is 1969 and America is at a white heat with energy. I flip on the radio, sample the channels for some report of the impending march on the Kremlin of the warlords, but find nothing except music.

Somewhere near the Ohio line I begin to notice vans roaring past with signs taped to the windows, and cars streaming down the lanes with hands waving. The moon is up and the land coated with light. The traffic thickens. I pull off at a truckstop, one of those official Ohio pit stops designed by government dullards. A couple of semis idle in the parking lot, but the rest of the area is packed with cars and vans. Inside, people stand shoulder to shoulder. I go to the restroom and the line for the urinals snakes out the door. People swap tales of the road, laugh about their impulse to go to Washington (it seems everyone in the nation made the decision the same way I did) and boast of the long drive they have already made. One guy takes the trophy by announcing his days behind the wheel from the Yukon.

The women behind the counter are angry. Their plain middle-aged faces contort with contempt for this bonanza of new customers. In part, the crowd has ruined the dead calm of the graveyard shift. But there is more to their reaction than that. They hate us, hate our hairy faces, hate the women with long hair and granny dresses, hate our army-surplus garb. They hate the fact that we exist in the same nation as they. Their Midwestern faces, properly lipsticked and rouged, hair in permanents, wedding ring and one small diamond on the left hand—their entire bearing is a mirror of the world that raised me and taught me the few values I know and believe. I have faced this contempt a hundred times, but the pain never ebbs. The truckers eye us like lice, and the sweet smoke of marijuana drifts across the formica tables like incense at a mass.

We drive on and rejoin the transcontinental conga line. In Washington, we crash on the floor of a house along the beltway, the panels of the family room echoing with television commentators toting up the score from a late night fracas between cops and demonstrators at the Vietnamese embassy on Dupont Circle.

We go to the hill. The halls of Congress seem under siege, the doors in the long corridors firmly closed. Senator Gaylord Nelson, a Wisconsin liberal, is open for business, however, and when we enter, his secretary is very polite and says, "of course the Senator will see you in a moment." I suddenly realize I have nothing to say. Standing in Washington is my only message.

This is America's City on a Hill. It just happens to be by a river in a bog. I cannot help but be moved by its feeble gestures toward empire, the architecture having been ripped off from schoolboys' dreams of Rome, the hands of the Founders in the radiating boulevards, monuments, and columns, columns, columns, everywhere these shafts of temples for dead gods. I was fifteen the first time I saw it, driving the old man's bread truck, sleeping on the street in Alexandria, Virginia, before a mansion where Lafayette had spent the night, my father getting up each morning, springing from his truck with the slop bucket in hand and strolling down the street to the nearest sewer hole. Monticello, the narrow stairways, the crazy beds in the walls, Mount Vernon with the key of Bastille framed and hung, the green dreams of the early Republic where a nation of yeomen would slowly sweep westward leaving farms and barns in their wake. I remember walking the mall at night as a boy, roaming the black district, hitching a ride and then sitting with my knife open on my lap. The crosses of Arlington cemetery.

My father takes me to the National Gallery, and we sit on a bench before Dali's rendition of the Last Supper. The glass of wine looks good enough to drink and the old man marvels at the red glow. He is wearing old slacks, a T-shirt, tennis shoes, and a wool shirt as a jacket. We leave, go down the marble steps, hit the sidewalk. The old man continues his celebration of Dali, wondering aloud how in the hell he could make a glass of dago red look so real. A bum approaches, says, "Sir, could I have just fifty cents for a cup of soup?" The old man pulls the hand-rolled cigarette from his mouth, snaps, "Fuck you," and continues his lecture on realistic values in painting. I am a believer and this peculiar city is the mother temple of my belief.

This time at the White House a circle of buses forms an aluminum barrier around the President who has announced he will skip the mass visit of his fellow citizens and watch football. I lie on the grass next to the Washington Monument, the sun dances across a sea of people, and long lines snake from the porta-potties. There are speakers and speakers and now and then a singer. There are 200,000 of us, 500,000, 750,000—the authorities will never agree on a number. We are the largest group of human beings ever to gather in protest in our nation's capital. The crowd is polite and limp. The music soothes, people talk and relax, the speeches drone on harmlessly. One television camera, from an educational television network, constitutes the sole coverage. This multitude has fallen through some hole in the communication grid.

I am not at ease. I dislike crowds. The light begins to soften as the afternoon advances, a faint breeze flutters the leaves on the trees. Suddenly, a splinter of ten or fifteen thousand people breaks off from the torpor around the monument. Banners wave in the air. A bounce enters the gait of the thousands streaming away. We join the group and advance toward the Justice Department. Various people have painted their faces or wear masks. This is SDS. Commerce, Labor, hulks of bureaucratic forts pass by. The group stops at Justice.

A rock flies, glass shatters, yells and chants fill the fall air. John Mitchell, the attorney general, stares down from the roof, puffing on his pipe. Cops arrive and encircle the crowd. We thread our way toward this blue border. I scan the cops. They are taking off their badges and I know it is time to get away. We slip through the line of saps and hard helmets. A moment later tear gas blesses the crowd. John Mitchell continues puffing his pipe, night falls.

For an hour we move carefully across the Mall while sirens shriek. Somewhere in the White House, I suppose, the President turns off his football game. We drive nonstop back to Madison, the tar strips between the cement slabs of the turnpikes going slup, slup, slup for hours. I know this will be my last march, action, demonstration. I go out in the garage and run my hands along the curves of the canoe.

Graves, tangle of forest, fat roots snaking across the ground, old stones leaning toward eternity, the dog sniffing the grass atop the ancient dead. From the dates, I conclude that this particular family arrived right after the War of 1812 when this section of the Massachusetts Berkshires opened up. A low rock wall surrounds the boneyard, the slabs with names and dates are thin and flat. The births begin at the time of the American Revolution and trail off on the eve of the Civil War.

The big black dog moves ahead into the trees. Job is a Newfoundland and fears nothing, explains nothing. He is one year old and just entering into the deeper fires of his blood. It is 1970. My boots scuff up the moldy cover of leaves, and the late fall air slaps my skin with warnings of winter. Stone walls lance through the forest, a legacy of old farms long abandoned. This patch of America peaked around 1830 and has since spiraled back into green, shadow and loneliness. When Crazy Horse was a boy and Custer not a general, American farmers mauled these hills, sucked warm juices from the earth, hacked the forests down, and devoured the meadows with the massive molars of their new cash economy. Then they fled West into first New York State and then the Ohio Valley and played out the same game again elsewhere.

The dog circles me and watches lest I escape. He moves indifferent to my commands—he recognizes no orders—but he will not let me leave his sight. He sleeps long hours, suffers no insults or unwanted visitors, and he always sniffs, taking long, deep lungfuls of air. He finds many messages on the ground.

A week after I arrived here in 1970, the sheriff descended to see if I might be harboring some fugitives accused of blowing up a building in Madison. Then everyone went away and kept their distance. The farmhouse sits on the end of a dirt road and no one has seriously worked this ground for several generations. This is promising country for anyone wishing to learn how to go slow. I can hear my heart drop its staccato, the spinning feeling leaves my mind, and I read no newspapers, listen to no radio reports, ignore all whispers of movement and change.

A neighboring farm has been converted to a snowmobile resort, and in a week or two when the snow flies, people will arrive from the cities, race drunk through the woods at night with headlights making bobbing stabs at the blackness. The packs of machines will sound like lawnmowers. The dog cannot abide these people and their machines. He will not let them touch one acre of the farm. It is night and he hears the engines, races off. I gaze out the frosted bedroom window and see a caravan suddenly stop as if facing the devil, then turn around. The dog returns and says nothing. His head is very large, the eyes brown, liquid, and sure. His feet are webbed. He seldom barks. He does not like noise. Or violence. He will permit no one to fire a weapon on his land. Once I fired a shotgun in the orchard and he looked at me with horror and betrayal and trotted back to the house abandoning me just this once.

Children are the exception to all his rules. He believes in their habits, high spirits and loud play. A baby crawls across the floor, slips its tiny hand into his huge mouth and pulls his tongue out. He does not stir.

We came here in September. A professor owned the farm and when the season ended, he fled like most of the summer people and left the ground to a winter guard. About a third of the local people thrive on welfare and the jukebox in the bar off the old village green belts out Buck Owens and the Buckaroos.

The house stretches aimlessly with many rooms. A huge kitchen hosts two stoves, one wood, one coal, and a walk-in pantry. The windows have many small panes and frame the gray skies into little snapshots. Just off the kitchen is a chamber that was once the borning room, a place where the lady of the house could recline near the end of her term and direct the cookery while she rocked with spasms of labor. Behind that is the workroom, two enclosed porches, an indoor privy. That is the first floor of the kitchen wing. The main hulk of the old frame building is two stories with a big attic, green shutters, four bedrooms, potbellied stoves. Beneath, a stone cellar maintains a permanent chill. Off the southwest, the two-storied barn and collapsing pump house show bare wood to the Massachusetts skies. This is the working core of a 200-acre farm where no one works. The lane leading up from the highway is lined with 200-year-old maples, each a couple of feet in diameter. The house looks down on an overgrown meadow, an orchard gone feral, stone walls slumping back to earth, and the eager forest that is slowly closing in.

During September, everyone in the surrounding area is cool, very cool. September does not prove anything. October is slightly better—as I buy a chunk of Vermont cheddar at the general store the clerk briefly smiles. When I ask for mail, the postmistress looks up. November does the trick. The neighbors, a couple in their sixties, suddenly appear in the yard, their truck sagging from the weight of an enormous old woodburning stove. They deftly install the black and chrome wonder, present my wife with a couple of geraniums to splash color from a winter window, and depart. Their people have lived on the road for 200 years. Yes, November is better. In November everyone realizes we will stay for the winter, for the real life of these ancient hills. The dog helps, too. Thirty miles away people know of the huge black dog that blocks the way of strangers probing this lonely dirt road.

My money is disappearing. I do not protest this fact. I seldom go to town, there is barely any television reception and few people care to visit from the Connecticut Valley once the hard weather settles in. I begin to slow down. My wife and I cease to talk of politics. Janis Joplin and Jimi Hendrix both die from bad habits and fast lives, a friend calls from Chicago suggesting a conspiracy, and I have nothing to say, really nothing to say. I read books, hundreds and hundreds of books. The books are very old and have a fine dusty smell. I find more in the attic and read them also. All of these books were written in the eighteenth or nineteenth century and I search for clues.

I walk often in the woods, the dog sweeping before me. Less of me comes back from each walk. I try to read *Walden* and fail. I make many small notes, then never look at them again. My wife loves the rich green of meadow under the electric glow of a threatening sky, the red of the autumn leaves.

There is an old stove down in the barn and I patiently restore it. The name and date emerge from a crust of rust. Stove polish brings up the glow of the metal. I buy stovepipe, install my work in a room and grin at winter. The barn is dark, warm and cavernous. The main beams were hand hewn on the place a century before. Old horse collars, rusty shoes, idle scythes, lazy shovels all lounge around in cobwebbed corners.

The orchard beckons and I scythe for days and slowly the pattern of the trees stands out against the carpet of green. Next I clear the meadow, a small thing of four or five acres. I enjoy sharpening the scythe against a stone. The dead fruit limbs I break up and add to my woodpile. When I look at the farmhouse from the meadow, the straight, rigid lines of building seem offensive against the soft curves and fluid textures of the forest. In the evenings, I sit on the stone steps of the house and watch the meadow sink into the dusk. Porcupines and woodchucks steal across the green carpet. Each morning a red fox cuts through the yard.

The house sits on a hill and below the trees take over and here in the bottomland I find the beaver ponds. They clog a small stream for half a mile or more. The stagnant water is studded with their houses and dams knife across at intervals. Along the bank, the saplings bear the mark of their teeth and the dog delights in rolling on their droppings. He swims in the ponds. We never sight a beaver, just hear the whomp! of their tails as we approach. I keep thinking I will go to the ponds without the dog, but this, I never do.

The rains begin in November and for thirty days the sun never appears. The leaves are stripped from the trees. Each day I walk a mile or so down the lane to the mailbox, amble past neighbors' farms, also idle, and count the barns weathering in the bite of winter. Buyers constantly come up the lane and try to buy the barns—the wood is esteemed as an element in the decoration of urban saloons.

I realize my time here will be short. I cannot afford to live as a gentleman farmer, and I lack the skills to live as a modern man of the Berkshires. I am here as a kind of retreat—I can see confirmation of this fact in everyone's face. I take what I can get. I want to go slow.

I cut wood all the time and size up the growing pile with hope. Then I section off and split the maple logs, glancing over my shoulder at the approach of winter. I knock down three times the amount of wood I think I'll need. When the snap finally comes, my pile lasts one month and I am fated to drag cords across the winter snows. One fall night I awaken to the honking of geese passing overhead on their way south. I stick my head out the window and am swept by a terrible feeling of loneliness.

The first snow falls in early December, the farm goes white, the paths and walls disappear under the drifts. Each week another foot or so falls and nothing ever melts. Barns begin to collapse and the locals announce this is the hardest winter in a quarter century. The dog and I travel the winter woods. We make no sounds. Our tracks cut the snow with clean, hard outlines. The dog enters into his country and I tag along. He stops at the stream, breaks the ice and swims. When he climbs out his fur flash freezes, the ice cracks and he trots along with sparkling sheets rattling all over his body. He refuses to sleep on the porch now and at night I scrape ice from the window and stare out at him snoring in the drifts. It is ten, twenty, thirty below zero and still the dog will not sleep inside.

After the first snow, the cat moves into the house. The dog and I have seen it in the woods a few times, a black and white blur darting away. The cat is feral and now it senses death in the winter sky and joins the family of man. I can tell from the cat's eyes that this decision sits sour in its belly. One day I hear a mewing in the cellar, go down and find it cold and starved. The claws flash, I cannot touch it. I do not know what to do. The dog does. Job refuses to eat and keeps nuzzling the cat. The claws flash again, thin ribbons of blood appear on his black nose. He continues to press his warm head against the freezing animal. Blood drips from him onto the floor. I whip up some oatmeal and lace it generously with maple syrup. The cat devours the bowl. Now the dog will eat his supper.

The pattern repeats each day, the nuzzling, the blood, then the cat feeding, and finally, the dog acknowledging his own supper. This continues for months.

January brings the hard cold. The dog now sleeps totally exposed, often on a bare rock. The cat has settled in and finds a good place to curl up in the cellar. One day walking down the lane to the mailbox, I fall and I think the world has become cement and will never be soft again.

Every day we wade through five-foot drifts to the beaver ponds. The air jells with cold and there are no sounds. I walk out on the ice and survey the buried kingdom of the beavers. There is a crack and then I go through. I feel nothing, it is far too cold for feeling. The dog plunges in, grabs my arm and pulls me toward firm footing. I flounder forward onto the ice, his teeth tug at my coat sleeve and I crawl on the belly to safety. My soaked clothing instantly turns hard with ice. Job breaks the trail ahead of me and I clatter along behind in the thirty below weather. I am wearing jeans, a shirt, a wool jacket. My body shakes. The dog keeps me moving ... he will not let me stop. I stagger a mile or so to the house, strip, fire up the stove and pour a shot of whiskey. Job sleeps at my feet. He has delivered and rids himself of any further responsibility.

Winter begins to release its grip in April and the mud season descends. The road goes bottomless and I must leave my truck a mile away. Water moves in a stream across the dirt floor of the cellar as the thaw gains momentum. There are porcupines everywhere and Job cannot get enough of them. I come home and he is sleeping on the steps, his face a forest of quills. I pull them out as he patiently sits there and then he goes off to find another one.

The cat strikes camp. I continue to set food out for her, the dog insists, but she eats it less and less often. Sometimes we run into her in the woods. I call and she runs over, tail wagging, and then she and the dog nuzzle each other. Each evening Job and I watch a woodchuck feed in the yard.

One day I find a porcupine walking across the meadow. I fall to my hands and knees and follow. The sun is spring warm, the grasses rank with scent, and the air is as fresh as the day the world began. For hours I crawl behind the porcupine. The planet is much larger this way and there is so much detail to confront and digest. The dog stays back and leaves me to my foolishness. I feel very calm and think nothing at all. The afternoon ebbs away and still I crawl and accept the gait of the bristling beast waddling across the land.

The train stops near the Moody Bible Institute on Chicago's near northside and the sun hovers, a pale disc, in the afternoon smog. Cold sweat pours from my body, my breath comes quickly—I have no control over it—and my heart pounds. I step out on the platform and assume I am experiencing a massive coronary. It is springtime and I have just left my students at the University of Illinois, Circle Campus. For weeks and hours I have marched them through the Salem witch trials, the Pullman strike, the Haymarket affair, the threat of Bauhaus to modern life. My classes cover a lot of ground and I am not very good at my job, teaching.

This rumble of a heart attack now apparently taking place in my chest, this big bang come home to roost, does not seem to disturb me. Some part of me considers it an honorable way out and at the very least a legitimate reason for a pause. Gradually my pulse slows, the sweats stop, my breath returns to a normal rhythm. It has been a false alarm, merely the fist of that new companion in America, stress. I touch the cold rail of the elevated station and feel reassured by the solidness of the metal.

The city takes me and I go down the stairs and into the street, an avenue thronged with winos. I walk over to the Newberry Library and sit in Bughouse Square, Chicago's historic shrine to free speech and mad hatters. I am twenty-five years old, an instructor in a university history department, and bored. No, not bored, sick to death. I have my routines, the work is light, the classes easy and I smell ruin at my shoulder. The white shirts, ties, tweed jackets, departmental meetings, small journals rich with type, all these things make me doubt myself. I should be grateful. I have found the good niche in the hard world. I feel like I have four flat tires.

I go home, load up the truck and beckon the dog. I drive hard until I get to the southern reach of the forest in Wisconsin. The dog bounds out and wanders off into the trees and I flop down on my face and smell the grass. I have walked out after one year of a three-year contract. I am finished in the higher learning. I have been bad.

The drive north is a drug. North Dakota, all green, wind-shaped and huddled under the force of the plains. I stop by a cemetery. Job races through the grass and I walk the small head-stones of hard Scandinavian lives squandered here wresting wheat from the angry skies.

As I plow north into Manitoba a gas station attendant cautions me to watch for moose on the night road. I have an uncashed paycheck in my pocket. The road stops at Flin Flon in the Ca-nadian bush. A friend teaches at a nearby Indian school housed in an abandoned DEW line station. The students are rounded up by airplane, imprisoned in the facility for nine months at a crack, and they spend the time with strong drink and some very good acid. My friend greets me with 1200 bottles of homebrew and a fishing pole. It is 1970, but the sixties linger.

Pike hit the Daredevil lures, we gut them, whack off filets, and curse the fat black flies. Sundown arrives around midnight, sun-rise an hour or two later. The beer supply never diminishes—we brew it in garbage cans. Everyone in the small village is drunk, all day every day. The woods stretch endlessly and the license plates boast 100,000 lakes. My friend counsels his charges on career plans.

I cannot stay. The bogs are pulling me down. I drive across the Canadian plains in a blur, see an elk in the Rockies, dive down into the valleys of British Columbia. The woman stands in a big garden, she has blonde hair, a wonderful smile, large breasts and no clothes. The commune has evolved from sixties dreams of escaping capitalism into early seventies demands of casting aside monogamy. This decision has caused a mass exit of most of the membership.

For dinner we eat a black bear that had wandered into the kitchen one morning. I sit in the evening with a friend who has fled California and the rigors of teaching philosophy in college. A loud wail of ecstasy punctuated by grunts rolls across the colony of A-frames as one of his fellow communards fucks his wife. My friend does not pause in his discussion of logical positivism.

At dinner near San Francisco, a woman I have known since I was a boy looks at me over her wine and considers my post in a modern university. I have not bothered to tell her of my flight. She says, "I never thought you'd settle for that."

The road ends in Arizona. I go to ground I understand. At the swap meet I run into Jake. We have not spoken in years. He is selling skins from Afghanistan, trophies from a long ramble through Europe, India, Nepal, Kabul, Laos, wherever. His eyes have gone hard, and the hair is flecked with gray. The acid plugs in and we go visit his shrink. She has a leopard-skin couch. I lie on a brass bed, the yellow metal tubes feeling like putty in my hands. We build a geodesic dome out of wood scavenged from the dump. I set up some beehives, plant a garden.

The call comes late at night and I go to the southside to the trailer. The door swings open, three guys stand around with rifles and shotguns, their T-shirts white, faces anxious. The load will arrive by truck in an hour or so. Construction has stalled in the city, they are masons and they need work. I give them the scales and leave.

The drugs are no good anymore. Jake and I hit a bar and the woman winces when he grips her too tightly during a dance. He has lost control. I drive home and the next day am reprimanded for traveling the sidewalks behind the wheel of a pickup truck.

A year or two later, I run into Jake on the street. He has just gotten out of the tank. He permits nothing but alcohol now, he explains. That way the images do not come.

It's not easy, he says softly.

I thumb the paperback book by the arched window and enjoy the morning sun. The old man is dying in the back room, I can hear his rough breathing as he struggles with the cancer that is eating him alive. The bookcase spills over with his legacy of Mark Twain, Charles Dickens, Gibbon's *Decline and Fall*, Cervantes' demented knight and fat sidekick. Outside the January sky warms as another desert day begins in Tucson. It is 1974 and the nation has slumped into the limbo of the seventies.

The end is very near now and I have come home for the finish. I sip weak coffee, perked. My mother prefers it perked, and the cup rests properly on a neat saucer surrounded by the frill of a doilie crocheted by her own hand. My father is almost eighty, my mother sixty and close to four decades of marriage reign in this house.

The book I hold is very odd, something by a man called H. T. Odum entitled *Environment, Power and Society*, a set of words sure to chill the heart and sedate the mind of any fun-loving American. I find it almost unreadable, but this is a time when almost anything can be read. The language batters me, the coined words, talk of feedback, amplification, gates, transformers, loops, kilocalories. Flows of energy seethe across the pages as hot rivers of life. I rub my bare feet against the nap of the nylon carpet, look up at a huge painting of the Old West, one complete with grizzled frontiersman, woman in bonnet, Conestoga, red Indian with skin oiled and shining in the desert sun.

I hear him stirring now, no, he is up, the feet sliding down the hall. I stand and walk over. He is on the march, the solid body shrunken, the legs incapable of lifting his feet, shuffling, scuttling down the hallway like a crab. He looks up and is angry at his humiliation. I ask him if I can get anything and he scowls and makes guttural sounds. The surgery butchered his mouth and throat and drool slides down one side of his face, the skin gray with a stubble of beard. He ignores me and slips past, weakly pours a cup of coffee, sits in the hard maple chair by the kitchen table and drinks. He cannot tolerate my help. This is the bond between us.

My mother sleeps in the bedroom, which is why I am here, so she can sleep while I take over a shift. Hospitals are out of the question. The old man does not countenance such places. I return to my book and scan the strange words: trophic, benthic, entropy. He is moving again, returning to his bed. The transistor radio fires up, a machine gun of words sprays the air. I walk back. He is sitting on the edge of the bed smoking a hand-rolled cigarette and taking in the latest gold report. He refuses to play the market any longer—he has doubts about the functioning of his mind now—but he keeps track and plays in his head with fake money. He is winning ... he always does.

The head is still held high, the thin gray hair sweeps over the well-formed skull, and the eyes are very clear and blue and hard. Not even terminal cancer can touch those eyes. Though all but mute, he is not silent. He scribbles messages on a small pad and grows furious when his handwriting is found all but indecipherable. The arms, legs and trunk have withered but the hands somehow retain their size and strength. To shake his hand is to deny his impending death. The market report ends, he snaps off the radio, takes a deep drag on his smoke and falls back on the bed. He ignores my presence.

Earlier I bought him some goose-down booties to warm his feet in this winter of his dying. They were large and puffy blue things, like slipping your feet into twin balloons. He rejected them out of hand as ridiculous and tossed them back at me. Another good sign. He refuses to be a patient. He would rather be dead.

A few days ago, the old man wanted something done and my mother could not fathom his croaks and sputters or puzzle out the increasingly loose scribble of his handwriting. He grew red and angry and motioned her over so he could speak in her ear. She bent down and heard this torrent of whispers, a phrase repeating over and over. She quickened, thinking this must be some endearment she must comprehend. Then the sounds suddenly became words in her head: "You think you're so fucking cute, you think you're so fucking cute."

The hours slide past, the sun goes white through the glass and I stay with my book. I have part-time work and a very big garden. I drink all the time and my insides seethe. My sister warns me of the awaiting ulcer.

The book warns me of Lord Kelvin's Laws of Thermodynamics. The world is energy and this movement can be sketched, measured and understood. I flip a page and examine a curious drawing, my first flowchart, a thing full of arrows, symbols, little notations of quantity and decline. The drawing is of a coral reef and the surrounding sea and I stay with it for two solid hours until I begin to understand. The book becomes my island in a house of entropy.

My heart is back in the desert now. I hear talk now that it is a very fragile place and that everything is really tied together in a magic weave called ecology. This is a new, distasteful idea to me. I came back to find the desert of my youth, the one where the gun sighted down on the deer, the four-wheel-drive truck roared joyfully through the wasteland, the place where you could always pitch an empty beer can out the window because there was so much of it that no human act could ever manage even to scratch it. I spend a night drinking with a man who was raised in Caborca, Sonora, an old mission town founded by the Jesuits and now plunging into large-scale irrigated agriculture as the final assault against the forbidding hot, brown ground. The guy is about thirty, Anglo, alcoholic and very smart. I tell him of this notion of the fragile desert and he refuses to accept this thought. He says he can take me places, secret places. We will get in his truck and go for days and then I will understand, then I will realize that the bulldozers, houses, farms, developers, bankers and slick magazine ads do not count in the long run. In the long run, he insists, nothing counts but the desert because it waits and it always, always wins.

We are sitting outside on the ground in the dry air of June. The traffic of Tucson purrs nearby, the fragrance of flowers floats through the rich darkness. June is always my favorite month here. The sun is relentless, no clouds interfere with the work of the desert and the light. The famous light that painters brag about, this light goes berserk, rachets up to some white blaze that flattens every object at noon and makes the entire city a paste spread out on the valley floor. In June, there are no doubts about this place. And the heat hits 105 or 110, metal things become dangerous to touch, the sidewalk cooks at an even 150 and everything is simple, honest and hot. Many people leave Tucson in June and only the lovers remain.

Where we sit in the dirt, the ground around us is littered with our empty beer cans and we see each other in the darkness at the glowing ends of cigarettes as the clock marches on midnight. He has been a dancer but now thinks he will be a sculptor.

The desert always wins, he repeats, always wins. He admits no doubt on this matter.

Using the techniques of the drawing of the coral reef, this idea of desert invincibility is translated into a swirl of numbers, arrows, and forms. The sun pours energy onto the land, rain comes and the plants blitzkrieg the surface with radical designs for capturing the solar largess. Storages of kilocalories dot the desert. Some sink from view as water into the earth, as dead leaves devoured by beasts, huge clumps of organic matter buried and rendered into oil, coal, shales rich with petrostocks. The whole image is connected with lines of force, a sun-created network of pipes, wires, and flows.

I close the book and examine my parents' home. The rug now becomes a sheet of fire fashioned from oil and for this moment called nylon. The hard wooden chair is a whimsy of sunshine from a distant forest. The coffee in my cup is a bean plucked by calloused hands in Brazil, steamed across blue waters to ports where English is the official tongue, then packaged, shipped, unpackaged and perked in a kitchen in Tucson, Arizona. And the old man choking on phlegm in his tortured sleep, the old man's body is acting out its last battle against Lord Kelvin's insight into the inevitable energy loss of any act. My father's body is slipping toward entropy.

I am alive with the force of the dull book. I begin to make new connections and with childlike pleasure seize a yellow legal pad and No. 2 pencil. The drawings are crude and my numbers feeble and inexact. I have a poor head for figures. But this does not matter at this moment in the house full of stale air and endless cups of coffee. I glance up at the cream-colored row of books by Mark Twain, the complete works picked up by father for a song, and I delight in thinking of all the kilocalories focused and dispensed through the simple lens of *Huckleberry Finn*. The world suddenly has a new form and any form will eventually convince the willing mind of its inherent good sense and elegance. I am that willing mind.

That night I sleep in my sister's old room, the walls and fixtures a gesture toward fine lines, frills and the dreams of a girl. She plays the piano and has an ear for the correct note. I am always suspicious of the correct note. The old man cannot sleep for very long periods of time and I hear him throughout the dark hours swinging his legs off the bed and sitting in the blackness, a hand-rolled cigarette burning between his fingers. I think of drawings, flows, a river of life that is indifferent and all but ceaseless.

I do not speak of these ideas to my father but I sense they will not be news to him. He was born with this knowledge in his bones. He has always operated like an animal, sniffing the air, eating the dirt, slyly opening himself up to currents that have no name but arrive with the spring winds. Nor has he ever doubted the chill of a late fall day. What I must learn from a book, he always knew. He could not die in a hospital. Such an act would be a violation of all he knew about life itself.

We once took trips together: I am fifteen and I drive the truck to Seattle—he does not say why. He sits in the back drinking, talking, drinking, sleeping, as the Great Basin flows past. We find an old hotel on the waterfront, he buys a bottle and retires to the room. There is no television, the window is open. He settles in. "The fleet is in," he notes, "the whole damn fleet." The street below swarms with sailors as night falls on the bars and dives. "Go," he says, "you are just young enough that they will not beat you—you're not worth a fight, you are nothing. See it, taste it, go." So I go.

The knife had cut months before. He walked into the building on a September day wearing a Stetson hat. I sat in the surgery lounge with my mother and eventually the call came. She felt like a small bird in my arms. The voice on the phone said the tissue was cancerous and that they must cut it out. She wept and then that passed and she returned to the routines of decades of marriage, thoughts of pulling him through surgery, of pulling him through therapy, of the menus she would plan, and small pleasures they would share.

He was four hours on the table, two hours in recovery and we did not see him until he was installed in the machinery of intensive care. He lay on the gurney and looked as small as a child. Tubes ran into his nose and veins, and his mouth was clogged with the apparatus of medical technology. He could not speak. I stared down into his eyes and for the first time in my life saw fear there, and pain. My mother patted his shoulder and made small sounds of comfort.

She turned to me and said, "Take his hand."

I groped under the sheet and found his fingers and palms. He squeezed hard, again and again. My mother and father ignored the small room full of hissing, blinking, wheezing machines. They were gray-haired, old, and yet reeking like animals in the throes of some deep biological act. I was the stranger intruding on an unspoken passion. The hours ticked off and eventually she tired and I sent her home. I elected to spend the night. Neither of us ever discussed leaving him alone.

Toward evening, the intensive care unit got busy with friends and family dropping in on the wounded. The lighting was kept low and the centerpiece was the nurses' station where rows of screens flashed with the heartbeats and data output of the dozen human beings wired into the ganglia of the machines. Visits were limited to five minutes an hour and the hostess met one in a long, almost formal dress. She had the manner of a greeter in a four-star restaurant, her hair long and blonde, the body tall and comely. I knew her from parties around town, the memory of a few shared joints amid the roar of rock 'n' roll.

By 10 P.M. the corridors emptied and the hospital grew still. I staked out a couch in the lounge and cracked a book on south-western archaeology in the 1920s. The blurry photos showed smiling women and serious men riding in tin lizzies, images of mummies found in ancient caves, of blank-faced Navajos helping with the pick-and-shovel work. The book had an orange cover, the language exuded the gay spirit of being young in new, wild country.

I would sometimes pace the halls of the big building and smell the cleaning agents that rose up from the slick linoleum floors. The doors and windows were all polished and every surface denied the pus, vomit, feces, urine and juices that poured daily from the faltering bodies of the inmates.

By midnight, I was alone except for a Mexican family from

some place south of the line. They watched television until the stations signed off and feasted on grocery bagfuls of chips, dips, lunch meats and soft drinks. They talked all the time and laughed a great deal. Every hour they would troop down to visit someone in intensive care, spend five minutes, and then return to the party time of the lounge.

Sometimes when I paced the halls of the hospital, I could hear the fluorescent lights humming.

I never slept. Each hour, I ambled into the half light of the unit, stood in the doorway of my father's cubicle and slipped softly up to the side of the bed. The room was almost dark and I could just make out his features from the faint light falling off the screens of the machines. I could hear his breath pumping through the whoosh of the respirator, watch his heart ping across the face of the scope that tracked the jagged rhythm of his blood. His eyes remained closed. I would speak quietly, touch him and then depart for another hour.

I finished the archaeological book by dawn.

He left the place four days later. They wheeled him through the lobby according to the hospital rules. Once outside the door, he dismissed the chair and wobbled toward the car. Once home, he walked into the kitchen, sat in his favorite chair by the table and flipped on the news. He said nothing, but deftly rolled a cigarette. My mother smiled.

Now months have passed and the game is almost over. The doctors found his body a sea of cancer and suggested he tidy up his personal affairs. He never speaks of this to me. He has always had a quick tongue and ready wit. His speechlessness is a great burden and he shuns company. But he makes no mention of this matter either.

I continue reading Odum, finish the book after a hard struggle, and begin again on page one. I am dumbstruck by the surge of life hidden under the wooden prose. Everything, the text explains, links up—the sun pours through the plants, the water powers the cells, molds the land, nibbles at the mountains. I stare out the living room window and catch the clatter of strategies sparring on the slopes of peaks, hear the merry thunder of my mother's roses.

I check on my father. He is getting over the anger of the bed, I think. My mother worried that in his growing weakness he might fall from the double bed she and her lover had always shared. I rent a hospital bed with metal rails on the side, cranks for raising, lowering, tilting. The old man flies into a rage, sputtering, drooling, finally scribbling note after note on this matter. I have violated his sporting interests: How do I know just how long he will live? What makes me so damn sure it is cheaper to rent than to buy? He will not give an inch. I stand in the smoky air of the back bedroom and watch the notes fall from his lap as he pens sheet after sheet of argument. He will not surrender easily to my judgment. He stares at me—I am not his son, I am a fucking punk.

He decides to put his affairs in order. I am leaning against the gray dresser. He sits with his legs dangling off the side of the bed and listens to the news report. He opens a drawer with effort, pulls out a roll of bills and peels off a hundred. Here. He shoves the money into my hand. Take this. Buy something.

I buy a backpack.

He takes no drugs, absolutely none. They might mess up his mind, he explains. I wonder about the pain but there are no messages concerning this matter. He is waiting and we both know it. My father has grandchildren and one, my sister's child, is less than one year old and very ill. The girl was born with a defective digestive tract and had a colostomy after six days on earth. This, the old man cannot abide. He cannot tolerate pain in any organism other than himself. Now a miracle operation is being performed to close the hole and restore her in her eleventh month to the normal world of diapers.

It is a Saturday and my father awaits a report on this surgery. The phone rings, my mother takes the message, walks back and tells him. The child will be fine she says. He weeps. Now he picks up his pad and makes a request: morphine. Finally, the morphine. I inject him, my first shot in this life. He is dead at 4 A.M.

I help carry his body out of the house. Then I clean up the room. I am determined to stop my mother from creating a shrine. I open the sliding door of the headboard on his bed and find two things: a loaded Army .45 automatic and a huge box of rubbers.

His ashes are scattered in the mountains. My mother hosts a party with meat, cheeses, all manner of food and drink. People sit in the backyard under the orange trees and talk and laugh and remember. The sun plays across their faces and they smile at my father's hard ways. Spring will be here in weeks.

I go to the desert more and more now. The landscape begins to look like an engineer's dream, a place of derricks, pumps, thick cables channeling sizzling energy. An antelope jackrabbit flashes through the creosote and I see the burning of kilocalories for the greater glory of the universe. I hike up to an old Indian spring near the village of Pan Tak, find potsherds littering the ground where generations of water carriers have stumbled. On the way back down I pass two desert tortoises standing motionless, one just in front of the other. They are panting and have just finished mating.

I am walking through the cholla and saguaro toward Baboquivari Peak, home of the god figure of the local Papago. I wear no clothes and the sun warms me as I slip through the curtains of thorns. The rock knob pulls me on and when I turn I see an entire valley of gears, engines, pulleys, levers, pumps, and contrivances devouring cascades of sunlight. I draw relationships on paper constantly, see explosive power stored in cultivated grains and for the first time in my life feel the almost thermonuclear result of human beings planting those rows of wheat and barley in the warm mud of Mesopotamia. All of history, all of politics becomes a sideshow for me compared to the real business of kilocalories flitting from here to there.

I enjoy the embrace of this monomania. I know it cannot last, that eventually all my drawings will become preposterous to me and go into the garbage. Ideas are made to be broken. But for the moment, I relish the experience. I keep rereading Odum's book and find a page where he has sketched the flows and kilocalories of heaven and hell.

Spring inches toward summer and I am administering a grant to create a conference on something about the Lower Colorado Basin. I scan my line budget, pick up the phone, and call Florida. Odum answers, thinks I am some kind of lunatic, and backs off. I keep calling. "Okay," he says, "I will come out."

He walks off the plane in a blue suit, white shirt, beer belly, scuffed shoes and white socks. The gray hair is careless, the face red, creased and animated. The voice belongs to the South. We go to the airport lounge, drink some beers and he begins sketching the energy flows of Arizona on a cocktail napkin. He has never been here before. His mind is like a psychosis … everything is grist for his vision. I realize he is the first genius I have ever met in a life cluttered with clever people.

He smiles and says, "I am glad to be here. I've never been in this ecosystem before."

I become obsessed with slowing the velocity of my life. I tend two bee hives and calm myself by witnessing the toil of tens of thousands of insects. The garden keeps enlarging and I hoe for hours like a monk deadening his soul to the devil's temptations. The alcohol continues to cascade through my body.

Odum smiles upon the industrial frenzy of the times. He scoffs at nuclear power plants as hopeless efforts to avoid the iron laws of thermodynamics, considers fusion an impossible dream and the enormity of our civilization a temporary binge. I ask him what will happen when the cheap stocks of oil and coal are gone.

"It's as much fun," he twinkles, "to march down the mountain as to march up the mountain."

I put him up at a guest ranch on the edge of the city. He wanders the ground clipping leaves, enjoying the architecture of cholla, smiling at the movements of a thrasher eating insects. He is like a child visiting a new amusement park. He argues that the mountains backdropping the city, the Santa Catalinas, are the community's greatest asset, the ultimate money in the bank. Over time they will pump more dollars, more kilocalories, more attention to this place than anything human beings can design. They are the General Motors of my town, he explains. He is quite serious, and immediately draws the whole idea on a sheet of paper, lines flying this way and that, energy tumbling through gates. "The mountain," he says, "the mountain, you can bank on it."

He begins to stay in his room and will not leave. He toils over his master drawing of Arizona, the entire economy of the state from the ecosystem's point of view. He works with fierce concentration and I peek over his shoulder as if I am witnessing Leonardo sketching his vision of flying machines.

I retreat to the resort's spa, a building with pool, sauna, and jacuzzi. At dawn I glimpse mule deer drifting up the wash. During the day a Cooper's hawk roars through the trees down near the stream, a snake glides through the tall grass. To the north, I can see the rock outcrop where my father's ashes are scattered.

Toward evening I take possession of the spa, roast my body in the sauna, plunge for laps into the pool, then sit for long soaks in the jacuzzi. By midnight the building is empty but I will not relent. There is a pop machine and it contains nothing but bottles of beer. I stuff it with quarters.

Odum is off somewhere transfixed by his drawings. I stretch out on a shelf in the sauna. The lights are off, a cold beer nestles in my hand. By 4 A.M. the jacuzzi demands more and more of my time. I set the timer again and again. The beer is now gone, the machine empty. The air of the big room sags with steam. I stagger out and march on the timer. The black knob rips from the wall and wires leap out into the air. The tub goes berserk, bubbling, roaring, and foaming without end and I let the waters pound my body.

Odum finishes his drawing and flies back to Florida. I scrutinize the lines and connections describing the movements and velocities that make up my ground. My father rides the winds of the mountain. I eye the $100 backpack on the wall of my room.

Clouds cover the sky like steel plate and the cold air hovers around thirty-two degrees. Winter is in the wind. I gaze down the careful rows and stitches of my blue sleeping bag. I have been in this valley for a day and I have not moved.

The surrounding walls are sheer rock. The stone is light in color, crumbles easily under the foot, tears off in the hand, the bad rock, the rotten rock. Crossing the Lechuguilla desert yesterday, the range rose up like a smooth, skinned beast. We came upon a steer that drifted north from Mexico. The beast had a puzzled look on its face in this dry desert full of spent shells and empty of water. I stretched out in the sand and made a cup of cocoa, the steer watching me with brute hope in its big eyes.

We paused at the base of the mountains near the tanks that give the Tinaja Altas range its name. Then we clawed and slipped up a side draw to this valley. We were very tired and did not want to make the climb. But it was necessary. I had to see this empty valley.

My face is blank, my eyes unfocused. A blur of ironwood, stone, and sand washes across my corneas. Thirty yards away, just past the lip of the cliff, the small puddles of water trapped in the rock extend down the mountain like a string of pearls. The water is green, cold and scummy. Hours ago, I looked down and then returned to the warmth of my bag. I am very still.

A row of spent rockets sits on a nearby boulder. They are toys left by the Air Force from their war games. Desert bighorn tracks dot the ground but the animals remain hidden from my gaze. I eat a bag of steaming freeze-dried food, shrimp creole today, drink a cup of black coffee. Then for two hours I recline and abandon all thoughts. I attempt to read but soon give up the effort. I expected this part to be difficult but giving up is a very easy thing to do in this place. The wind whips across the tiny hollow, sounds flutter off the rocks.

A golden eagle lands near the lip of the cliff, the huge wings extended, the feet splayed outward. The feathers fold into the brown body, the bird falls still and stares at me. I return the stare. I am very excited, the huge predator is so close, the eyes are so sharp, and then my excitement subsides and nothing is left but the eagle, my body, and the blue nylon bag. We both drift into our own thoughts. Mine are empty of real thought.

Minutes tick by, the sky remains as hard as boiler plate. The eagle lifts off and drops below the cliff to course the valley.

I make no notes.

**The man under the ironwood tree beckons, his hand
extended, fingers pointing down to the ground and
flapping.** This is Sonora and the gesture means come over.

The fire crackles under a sheet of tin and the coffeepot bubbles with hot water, the blue metal blackened by smoke. Six
campesinos huddle in the chill of a January day in the mid 1980s.
Their brown hands show work and the smiles reveal teeth missing here and there. I am only a few days into the long march and
my body aches. The back of my left knee drips with ooze and
blood. Yesterday, while walking the tall grass along the desert
river, a downed swirl of barbed wire wrapped my legs. I fell like a
tree, the sharp spines of metal dug into my flesh. When I looked
at the wound I saw sinew and muscle popping out of a deep hole.
Bill Broyles hobbled over through the rank growth and went,
tsk, tsk, tsk. Then he shifted easily into his paramedic mode,
wrapping the gore with a dressing. This I could not abide. The
thing itched and begged for air. So after an hour or two I ripped
the tape and cotton off and now I have this oozing hole. When I
peer into the flesh, I see odd, thin fibers of muscle and they bulge
out like a hernia. The wound is covered with dirt but somehow
I know this does not matter. The wire was old and rusted and I
have no up-to-date tetanus shots, but I sense this also is of no
account.

We are going to walk hundreds of miles through empty
country and a hole seeping blood under my kneecap becomes

a detail. Bill and I keep returning to this place because almost no one else does. It is hot, hard, bare, and in the eyes of most people, ugly.

The black rock breaks the shackles of my humdrum mind and I drift. I am sitting at a table in a bar in South Tucson working out the genealogy of the local narcotics trade. The man eyeing me has fifty years on these streets and contempt for the possibility of change. He speaks cryptically while the cooler roars through a vent over his head. We drink Nude Beer, the latest wonder from Mexico—scratch the label with a coin and a bare-breasted blond emerges to grace the bottle of suds. I rattle off names, he nods, glowers, tosses out vague tips. I drain my bottle and he looks at me with scorn and concern. "I know who they are," he snorts, "I know what they are, and I stay the hell away."

It is better in the black rock.

The campesinos around the fire show interest in our appearance. We are white, dressed in shorts and T-shirts, filthy from sleeping on the ground and avoiding soap and water, and we carry these enormous bags on our backs as if we were poorer than the poor, men too far gone to have a horse, mule, or burro, men who themselves are nothing but beasts of burden.

They offer the cup and I take its warm metal into my hand. The sides are gray, the lip blue and inside leaves swirl, perhaps pieces of ephedra, Mormon tea, the brew of the desert's lean and hungry people. I swallow and feel the warm rush of mezcal and smile. The men smile back with the force of a sudden gale.

I have no bad memories of this mezcal, the bootleg booze of Sonora. Peasants in the lower Sierra Madre scout out the right agaves, and distill this wonderful liquid. I have lain on the black rock past midnight drinking cup after cup of this mezcal, stars shouting overhead, the desert whispering rumors of death, the talk loud and freewheeling and all the memories fresh and within reach. I remember one night by a huge black crater in the Pinacate when a friend, a man of seventy some years, thought of his dead, beloved wife and swung his cup of mezcal toward the heavens and said, "I will never stop believing. This cannot end." And I knew he did not mean that there had to be life after death or that the universe had some fixed meaning but simply that a love as fierce and good as he had shared, that such a bond never ceased and the corruption of the flesh and the march of time were small matters in the face of such a feeling. Mezcal, always the right drink.

The men huddled around the fire have a big bottle sitting out on the ground and they circle the smoke on small folding chairs and enjoy the day before a hut of sticks, cardboard, scavenged wood and sheets of tin. They are members of Ejido Cerro Colorado, a tiny sliver of the Mexican land reform program that is a gesture toward giving peasants a patch of earth. The ejido is more than twenty years old and sited by an often dry river in a hot desert. The men are very proud of their communal home. They carry two chairs over and insist that we sit, but we politely refuse and stand there sipping mezcal with our warehouses of backpacking gear straining at our shoulders. We know if we take the loads off and settle into the mezcal, we will be finished for hours and then night will fall and we will wake up by the cold embers of this friendly fire.

Past the hut, a bosque of mesquite hugs the river and beyond the trees, a thin trickle of water rides above the sands for a short ways … a few miles further down it will disappear into the earth. For days we have been greeted by great blue herons rising off the scummy stretches, the huge wings slowly beating against a landscape of cholla, saguaro and bare ground. One morning I see a kingfisher sitting on a limb and here and there clouds of pupfish storm across the skin of moisture. The men do not talk of the birds.

They wish to know the pattern of our journey, what sierras and *despoblados* we seek and they smile approval and laugh at the scale of our hunger for ground. They do not walk for pleasure.

At first I sip the liquor and then take big, hearty guzzles of mezcal and eye the sun blazing through the glass of the clear bottle. This walk is a tactic to control the speed of things bashing around me. All my walks seek to stop the noise in my head. A man sits across the table in a Tucson cafe, his shirt half open, the suit very high quality, the hair razor cut. Gold chains hang from his neck, thick gold rings ride like blobs on his fingers. He is in the traffic—the word on the street is that he is very hard and not a man to deceive or cheat—but we do not speak of this fact. He has a four-hundred-pound problem—they opened the trunk, what can one say?—but this too slides past as a trifle. He locks his fingers together, pulls with anger, all the while smiling. He hints at what he would like to do with an adversary. Then we order.

I intend to slow down until the earth itself stalls my drive and then I will melt into the ground. Bill and I have sketched out a path that runs more than two hundred miles. We will retrace the route of a dead Norwegian, Carl Lumholtz, a man who in 1909 came this way. We have a detailed map in our packs that records his passage through the Pinacate and Gran Desierto of northwest Sonora, a pan of black rock and white light edged by a blue ocean. The map shows the land as white, the mountains gray, the sea blue, a warm, rich blue, and a thin red line going everywhere and labeled author's route. We follow that red line like dogs on a strong scent. The trail is cold now, three-quarters of a century cold, but this hardly hinders us and as the days pile up, this wall of decades will become a detail. Time does not matter here.

The gift of mezcal in the big mug strikes me as close to my purposes. We are standing with six peasants before a hut by a desert river and sharing their liquor and the good time of their afternoon. My backpack costs more than their entire estates but this does not seem to matter to any of us at the moment. Mexico can be like that at times, strangely forgiving of the canyons between rich and poor.

For days we have passed homes where the windows lacked glass and now we see huts that lack windows. The men with the mezcal dispel this feeling of poverty. They say, come back in the spring, come back then and see the ejido blossom with life and people. They fish in their pockets and one man shows an agate, another a turquoise. The blue stone flashes against the brown hand.

We sleep that night on a salt flat, Agua Salada, under a hungry moon. I am restless and toss on the hard ground. The soil is crumbly kernels of salt, a pavement of white punctured here and there by mesquite. I am not an outdoorsman and am completely dependent upon the high-tech toys in my backpack—the knives, packets of food, ingenious stoves, lanterns and feather-weight flashlights. I do not know how to use a compass, cannot set a broken leg, and view snake bite with fatalism. I outfit myself with running shoes, running shorts and tend to wear the same T-shirt for weeks. I know no knots, cannot identify edible plants and have not killed and then eaten an animal for more than ten years. I read few books about nature and kind of shudder when I see the word, particularly if the first letter is capitalized.

The palo verdes sway in the breeze, birds dart with lust through the thorny limbs. I am sitting on the steps of my new office building along River Road, the design a cheap knock-off of an imaginary Sante Fe. The man speaks into my recorder with a monotone. When I replay the tape, I can barely hear his voice above the whispering of the wind. He is talking about his hikes. It is 1966, he is behind enemy lines in Cambodia. What did he do? "I interrogated prisoners," he says. Sometimes at night, he says, his wife finds him in the corner weeping. His hiking occupied three years. He became adept at outdoor skills.

The night air flows like lead down the river bottom crushing the salt flat along the Sonoyta. I pull my head and shoulders out of the bag and lean against my backpack. Bill sleeps soundly, and I listen for the pad of a coyote.

We awaken at first light, make coffee, watch the gray leave the sky. That morning we pass the last hut along the river, a small rancho with beef jerky and snakeskins hanging on a clothesline. Smoke from a mesquite fire bites our eyes as an old yellow dog worries us along. The family—a young girl, a boy, a man in his early twenties—poses for a picture against a blank wall. They do not ask why.

We leave the river at a patch of dry sand called Agua Dulce and knife fifteen miles across a creosote flat. The vegetation is monotonous, the wildlife absent from my eyes. Lumholtz rattles around in my head and will not tolerate bad talk about such a vista.

"Though strictly speaking," he shyly admits, "nothing in nature is ugly, the greasewood could not be called beautiful.... It may be compared to a person radiant with health and good cheer, for which he is liked, though he may not be handsome. Were I a poet, I should sing the praise of the modest greasewood of sterling qualities."

I think the old Norwegian is trying too hard, but he has a point. Toward noon the stillness of morning ends and a faint breeze begins to swish through the slender limbs of the greasewood. The sound is low and frail and very comforting. As I walk I pull clumps of the oily leaves through my hands and smell the pungent odor. Scientists have determined that creosote lives a very long time, perhaps more than 10,000 years. The small shrub somehow sterilizes the soil near itself to keep other plants' seeds, and its own, from taking root and the foliage reeks of such distasteful chemicals that no grazing animal is likely to munch on it.

In the beginning the creator walked this ground, drew greasewood from his heart, and used the staff to aid his passage through the darkness. He made ants also and the ants climbed his stick and fashioned a round ball from the gum of the wood. The creator stood on the ball and sang,

I made the world, and lo!
The world is finished.
Thus I make the world, and lo!
The world is finished.

So say the Piman people who under various names once clotted this desert with life. Lumholtz, despite being a hardball naturalist, explorer, ethnologist and man of science, buys into these old myths. So do I. He is a fine companion for this walk.

He is forty-nine years old and has just survived a bad bout of dysentery. The bug nailed him to a sick bed in Magdalena, Sonora, during the annual fiesta of San Francisco and for days Lumholtz wrestled with the spasms of his colon and had to endure, he laments, "two monstrosities of merry-go-rounds of the most prosaic American manufacture, with mechanical devices for the accompanying noise of horribly loud organs." But normally, he is a good traveler. As a young man he tackled theological studies in his native Norway, broke down, fled to the forests and eventually obtained a Master of Arts degree from the University of Christiana. He decided to devote his life to exploration, plants, animals and other cultures.

"The beauty of nature took hold of me," he confides, "and I felt my freedom from the confinements of metaphysics and scholasticism. I was overcome by emotion and wept from joy."

At age twenty, he roams the outback of Australia and lives with blacks along the Herbert River, dining extensively on the local cuisine. "The large lizards," he recalls, "should not be despised, but the flesh of snakes was dry and practically unfit as food, though the liver is pleasing." He beams with pleasure over the memory of the tangy, toasted larvae of a large brown beetle.

Now he crosses the same long creosote valley as Bill and I. He is outfitted with figs, dates, shelled fruit, bacon, honey, flour, horses, mules, burros, a wagon, three Mexicans and three Papagos. One of the Indians is a shaman. The Mexicans and Papagos are puzzled by Lumholtz and cannot understand why for days at a time he stays in his tent scribbling, scribbling, scribbling. Bill and I are little puzzled by this behavior ourselves. At first we both kept busy filling notebooks and would whip them out at the slightest pause for an orgy of penning fat entries. As the days drift by our notes grow thinner and then spotty and finally get forgotten. Coyotes howl, stars work the sky, ravens swoop over our bedrolls at dawn. We put our pens away.

I am sitting on the ground eating a granola bar near the lip of the Pinacate lava flow. The area is 750 square miles of black rock with no living water. The lava rolls over the land with knife-sharp edges. An ironwood stands gray-green and light washes everything with a clear rinse. Nearby, an ancient Indian trail arcs through a low saddle. I feel a little lonely for the hubbub of the greater world. Lumholtz considers such feelings and advises me that "for the first days or weeks one misses sorely one's mail, especially if interested in knowing what took place on the rest of the globe, but after a while one gets used to being without news." I suppose.

I hear a hissing sound that grows louder and louder and look up to see a dark dot cutting huge oval tracks against the blue sky as a hummingbird roars through its courtship dance. A cheap digital watch flashes time on my wrist. I listen to the dance of the bird.

I am in a bar at the Westward Look planning the prototype of a magazine. The blond woman has spent her life in Tucson and warms to the task. She says, "Call it 'Speedway'" and words pour out about the joys and fears of Saturday night cruising in high school. I am bewitched by the word, "Speedway, SPEED-WAY," and envision white line fever all over the pages. We finish our drinks. Her voice sings in my memory with the excitement of teenage nights and hot summer air pouring through the open car window, the radio bathing life in a safe, steady beat. A year and a half later she is found raped and strangled in her new townhouse. The police say they have no suspects.

We make camp on the lip of Vulcan Elegante, a big crater. Another Indian trail circles the giant hole and at points there are remnant blinds where men once huddled and waited with sharp spears for the passage of a bighorn sheep. Lumholtz is seized with the desire to know the exact circumference of the caldera, mounts his mule and rapidly trots the circuit, timing his lap carefully so as to calculate the distance. I smile at his dedication to science and sprawl on the ground. Nearby a brittlebush shelters against a black boulder. I do nothing at all but look at the gray leaves and yellow flowers against the dark rock. I do not throw my aesthetic feasting up to Lumholtz with his exact notes about meters, kilometers, hectares and degrees Celsius. Of course, he cannot be dismissed as simply a creature of science.

"Love of nature," he whispers, recalling his youth, "took stronger and stronger hold of me and one day it occurred to me what a misfortune it would be to die without having seen the whole earth. I could hardly endure the thought which haunted me."

The mule is sweating from a brisk trot around the crater and the Norwegian looks like a big load for the poor animal.

The next day Bill and I head for Tinaja Emilia—Lumholtz picks the name, some lady friend of his in Boston—and find the lava blocking any direct march. We are forced to detour through the ancient water hole at Suvuuk. Trudging along a thin wash, we spook a great horned owl from an ironwood and the big bird flies uneasily across the brilliant noonday landscape. Suvuuk is dry, as usual, and we follow a jeep road up the bajada toward the mountains. One flat stretch is a favorite of airplanes making unannounced landings in the Pinacate drug-smuggling industry.

I pause on the straight dirt stretch and listen for the shrill voices, voices like cicadas in the frenzy of summer, of stockbrokers in New York, high-strung lawyers in Los Angeles, all manner of urban wildlife begging for the magical white powder. It is a basic component of my city now. I remember a woman telling me of visiting a friend from high school. He told her of looking up two buddies from their class and finding them residing in a small southern Arizona hamlet. Guns were out in the open and the next room held a million dollars worth of cocaine. I listen for the hungry rumble of a twin prop aircraft. And then we exit this node of North American commerce.

At Emilia there are green pools of water, tanks of fluid captured by holes in the rock during the infrequent rains. Mosquitoes sing in our ears and sleeping circles left by ancient hunters dot the lip of hill over the wash. Lumholtz writes all this down and his men kill bighorn sheep to break the monotony of camp fare. The Norwegian has these mixed feeling about Indians, at times critical of their reluctance to join his machine world and then again bewitched by their links to the wild places.

"In regards to man's relations to nature," he decrees, "the Indians have since the discovery of America learned nothing and forgotten nothing and it will take many centuries to change their mode of thinking."

We go up the mountain the next day. Bill finds a ram's horn with a good curl and we tote it along. We climb down into a volcanic tube; the roof has collapsed and created a big skylight. The Papagos call this I'itoi's cave, one of the homes of their god figure and guardian. Back in the darkness, I find bones littering the floor. I reach up on the black wall and carefully place the ram's horn as an offering. Lumholtz and his Indians are singing nearby. They have brought an offering of blue beads and eagle feathers.

Carrion Hawk, an old shaman from Quitobaquito near the border, has not been here in many years and he is alarmed at the changes in I'itoi's house. It seems the roof has collapsed more than he remembers. Is Elder Brother happy?

I watch bees work big white combs that hang like drapes from the ceiling. The silent bones clutter the still dust of the floor. A long time ago the people came to I'itoi and complained that the mountain stood so tall that the sun was blocked and the days were much too short. The god whacked the peak down and the rubble of lava, the open sores of craters, the flats of cinders, all these things mark the ferocity of that act. Carrion Hawk prays to I'itoi and I think Lumholtz is kind of touched.

"I did not come to visit you," the old Indian confesses, "because the weather was bad.... A man comes here from the other side of the sea to know your house. I bring him and his companions from Sonoyta. Give good luck to the man and to us all.... Stop the wind."

A golden eagle drifts far below, studying the dark rubble for some flicker of life that it can kill. Hours later we reach our camp. All the food is scattered, the bags ripped to shreds. I crawl across the ground in the wind grubbing sunflower seeds, peanuts and raisins. A krawk! krawk! cracks over my head and I look up to see two ravens hovering ten feet above.

The sun goes away for days and gray clouds pour in from the sea. The air hangs heavy, light rains wash across the Pinacate and the black rock glistens. We follow no trail and blunder cross-country, swinging south and then west around the mountain. The washes become small canyons, silent and empty with big ironwood huddled in the drainages. One day we tumble down a rock wall and find an abandoned Indian camp. The small stove hisses and we savor hot chocolate among the broken pottery fragments. I read Frank Norris' *The Octopus* by candlelight and there is no mail. We see no one, hear no machines, not even a plane whirring across the soggy sky.

Our bodies grow eager for the packs and there are no questions of pace or route. There is very little talk of any kind and we move over a big piece of flat ground, the small stones punching through our thin soles and bruising our bones. Bill stops, stoops down, picks up an elegant arrowhead, and we walk on with no words. The clouds drop low, scudding over the land and the mountain vanishes. Cool breezes chill our bodies, the raindrops tingle on the face. Each night coyotes howl and then at gray light there is the dawn song and black coffee.

We find stone outlines of animals on the ground, big reliefs sketched by neolithic artists in their idle hours. I crawl into small rock overhangs and lie on my back to see paintings safe from museums. Sometimes we sit for hours by a water hole and listen to bees, watch birds drink, wait for nothing to happen minute by minute, day by day. At night I have no dreams and do not wonder at the stars.

A sharp rock rips the seat of my shorts and I patiently sew up the tear. The stove breaks. Bill fixes it. My abandoned notes get wet in the rain and I marvel at the forms made by the running ink and finger the soggy paper. Lumholtz is in a state of constant delight, identifying plants, eating local treats brought to him by the Papagos. His animals begin to fail, the horses first, and he learns with time that only the burros are made for this country.

To the west, we see the wall of the dunes, mile after mile of sand restless under the winds. We march along between this yellow horizon and the black up-sweep of the mountain. The ancient Indian camps and rock outlines of beasts, the old trails and paintings break up our days. I recline in the sacred places with the dead gods.

The divine presence changes with time. A tall blond serves the drinks in the bar on Miracle Mile, Tucson's persistent belt of popular vice. The man speaks to me of scholarly matters—urbanization, water laws, the morphology of human communities. The speech is quick, almost frantic, as if there were no idle moments left on the planet. Every ten or fifteen minutes, he excuses himself to use the phone. He sniffles a great deal. And then one of the phone calls works out and he must leave. Right now.

The low clouds continue and they wrap us with the breath of the sea. I look down at my feet and see a control panel. Cutouts for toggles and dials stare from the metal sheet like eyes and there is the word RADAR. Wires trail delicately across the hard ground. Next come pieces of aluminum and toward nightfall sections of the fuselage and a door. A decal recommends the use of thirty-weight oil and suggests checking the amount regularly. The sun peeks through and gleams of metal blaze among the black lava.

Several years ago, a plane purred overhead carrying two American couples bound for a vacation on the beach. I imagine laughing men and women dreaming of cold drinks on the hot sand and nights of love. The plane exploded, the brilliant fragments cascaded to earth, the bodies hitting with a pulpy thud. The charges had been set by radio and each wing was neatly sheared off. The pilot had flown often between Mexico and the states and there was speculation that he had erred in his conduct during some transaction.

A campesino prospecting in this remote area witnessed the free fall from the sky. He showed up at a rancho to the north wearing a nice watch and with flashing rings on his fingers. He bragged of having intercourse with one of the corpses.

Lumholtz considers other debris. One of the Mexicans hands him a human scapula. The head, he learns, is missing but many other bones remain, plus pieces of a gray felt hat, scraps of black cloth and a can of baking soda. The Norwegian is intrigued. "Another report," he grins, "was brought to me that the 'professor,' meaning myself, had also died from thirst, and that the coyotes had dragged away his head." Lumholtz fingers the bone. The Mexican calculates the headless skeleton has waited in the sands for a decade.

The sun is fully out now, a ball of fire nestled in the drift of clouds and Bill and I walk along in the strong light. We have come a long way up the west side of the Pinacate and we know the silence will soon end. The ground begins to show the mark of cattle, little dry piles of dung, dirt trampled to fine dust, plants half mutilated.

That night we camp near a collapsed volcanic tube. I drop down in the hole, find signs of guano and a few spent cartridges left by some bravos who amused themselves by spooking the now absent bat colony. I climb out hand-over-hand and sit on the hill watching the sun sink into the sea. Behind me scraps of aircraft flare in the red light and I think I hear the happy laughter of a Mexican prospector. Lumholtz is a child in this landscape. He drips with joy over the mountains marching across the desert flats. The whole empty region tugs at some deep part of himself.

"Could I select the place," he says in a soft voice, "where I should like best to die, my choice would be one such as this. I hope at least it may not fall my lot to pass away in New York."

I watch the light vanish from the skin of the dead airplane. That night Bill and I hardly speak. We know what we will find tomorrow because we also have received reports. A few months before Bill drove up to a water hole in the Pinacate. Men strode out from under the ironwoods, automatic rifles with long magazines cradled in their arms. Big trucks were parked and hidden under the trees. The men were not friendly and announced they were cattle inspectors for the Mexican government. Later, Bill approached the spot on foot under the cover of night. He must have hit some trip wire . . . suddenly shots were fired into the blackness.

An Indian comes to Tucson and tells me he has been offered $5000 to drive a truck from the line north to Chandler, a town near Phoenix. From time to time, he hauls cargoes of illegal aliens, and he is never paid that kind of money. He does not ask what this load will be. A customs agent is killed on the reservation. The papers say the murder was done by drug smugglers from Mexico. A friend tells me, no, that is not it, it was some guys out on the rez who got mad about a deal. After the killing they drank for a night and talked it out and then it was history, a finished thing. Everyone knows, he says, but it does not matter. It is simply part of the business. I nod. Yes, it is a finished thing.

We are in the Pinacate on a different trip and walk across a flat clearing. The desert pavement with its coat of varnish flashes in the sun. Two parallel rows of rocks march along outlining an airfield with a neolithic look.

I am sitting outside a Mexican cafe a half mile south of the line and trying out my feeble Spanish on the cook's helper. Across the road is a shrine on a small knoll, the path to the statue glittering with the broken bottles of many happy beers. At night small aircraft fly over the cafe and they fly very low and head north into the desert emptiness of the United States. The man I am talking to, and others from the cafe, work part-time in the Sierra Madre harvesting the crop, and they receive $250 a week plus board. And to the south there are those airfields and men with rifles and sometimes these men come to the cafe and no one asks, no one asks a single question. Caborca, a farm town left as a legacy by Father Kino, is the new, bustling center of this trade. There is a street in Nogales, quite near the fence, where armed men block entry to those unwanted. The successful men who live along this street, a friend tells me, do extensive re-decorating—they demand heavy drapes. Everyone along the line is very much afraid.

Bill and I sleep a few miles south of the water hole where he encountered the peculiar cattle inspectors and a few miles south of a big ash flat where the sound of airplanes often shreds the night quiet. I do not care. I absolutely do not care. This problem is past the reach of law and buried deep in human appetites and human fears. I watch the stars slowly arc across the heavens hour by hour and feel the cold pour against my skin. Lumholtz is over in his tent making detailed notes on that human scapula.... I can see the glow of his lantern against the canvas walls.

We move at first light and hit the ash flat in the heart of the day. At one edge is a small rancho and we hesitate at the fringe of trees lining the huge opening. Then we march straight across the pan of dirt and small stones. I can feel eyes watching us as we lurch under our heavy packs and when we reach the far side, we amble up to a big ironwood, toss down our loads and bring out some salami for lunch. Grease glistens on the blade of my knife as I cut through the thick, oily meat. Six miles to the east, the Sierra Enterada, the Buried Range, chokes in the sands of the dunes. Nearby is the Sierra Extraña, the Strange Range. This has to be the proper spot.

It does not take long. I look up from my lunch and see our visitors arrive in a flatbed, the cab a light blue. One man stays in the truck and smokes and does not smile. The other hops out, hitches up his pants, a huge silver buckle riding like a jewel under the expanse of his gut. He walks over and does not offer us cups of Mormon tea powered with mezcal.

Lumholtz is oblivious to all this. He is entranced by a mockingbird, "who has evidently never seen people before ... passing my camera within four feet." The bird lands on the toe of one of his Mexican helpers and the Norwegian is delighted by such bravado.

The man from the truck has questions: Who are you? Where have you come from? Where are you going? Why are you here? His voice pounds out the words like a hammer and the eyes sit deep in his skull. We tell him about our friend Carl Lumholtz but the man professes ignorance of the famous Norwegian scholar and explorer. It is pointless to mention the curious behavior of the mockingbird. The creature lands on the rim of a large dish and repeatedly dips its head into the water. Lumholtz cannot contain his pleasure and keeps snapping photos.

Bill chats about our journey and the beauty of the desert in winter. The man does not smile at this recitation of our adventures. The fine midday air droops with menace. We have heard talk of the man with the fine belt buckle. Lately, he has appeared in a nearby border town with a great deal of money in his Levi's, more money than the wildest dreams of cattle sales could ever produce. Bill, out of politeness, does not inquire into the state of the range this year and the prospects for marketing steers. Lumholtz has stopped his picture-taking and is busy making notes on his wonderful experience with the mockingbird. The man stands planted in his boots and has no small talk.

The truck leaves ... apparently this matter can wait for a while. Bill and I pack up and disappear into the roadless sands, making an almost invisible camp against the embrace of the Strange Range. Lumholtz cannot stop, he is intrigued by the presence of badgers miles from any water. Low clouds creep across the desert that night and at dawn a light rain falls. We do not say much about the man and the light blue truck and the big ash flat that is so superb at hosting large, powerful flying machines. Bill is disturbed by the presence of commerce in this place. He says, "I don't like people messing up my garden."

I am less certain. I am losing my ability to keep things in what is considered their proper place. My desert and the gears of my city and the machine age increasingly touch and merge in my mind. I want the desert pure and sacrosanct, but I must confess my own needs and nature. I am a city man and I live off the stress the city gives to me and I cannot imagine life without this tension prodding me to act, think, and hopefully, change. The desert, the big empty where human beings do not dominate, is necessary to slow down my velocity, to rid the clutter from my brain. But it is too late for me. I am too long out of the stone age and I can only visit the past—I can never live in that country.

My pulse quickens at the thought of trucks rumbling down the backroads in the night, sweaty men unloading cargoes while their comrades stand by with rifles at ready, small aircraft revving engines and then vanishing like swift birds in the blackness. I think of the man in the Tucson cafe, the gold chains, good suit, ready smile. The way his hands gripped each other for emphasis.

The light rain stops and we hike over to the Buried Range. I lie on a rock and stare off into the sea of dunes. A falcon glides overhead and then suddenly a second hunter drops from the sky and dives with talons extended toward the back of the other bird. One flees.

We zigzag north and wind through the dunes. Rodent tunnels undermine the sandhills and we stumble hour by hour. Burrowing owls stand and bob among the light clumps of dry grass and thorny bramble. Lumholtz decides to leave us here. His pack animals do not savor the poor footing. And he is about other errands. He must find more unexplored country. He talks up Borneo and is mesmerized by the thought of New Guinea.

"Among people who know," he thunders, "it is the universal verdict that no region offers such inducements for exploration as New Guinea."

He will die in 1922 but of course he does not know this now. He is busy planning because he will never rest easily in the civilization that is raking the globe with machines and orderly practices. I suspect that given the gear he would flee to other planets. Nearby is a big crater where, in 1972, American astronauts trained so they could get a sense of the surface of other worlds. Local vaqueros remember them as *"los hombres de la luna."* The Norwegian cannot wait for such options, so New Guinea it must be.

Lumholtz pushes off, the men and beasts trailing away into the late afternoon light. Bill and I camp just below the crest of a dune on the forgiving sand. The sun drops like a red rock and I look up as an owl slips past my face four feet off the ground. The bird is a silhouette against the dusk and the wings never move as it hunts the dune. Nearby I can see trucks rumbling along the two-lane highway that hugs the border and links mainland Mexico with the bare finger of Baja. The machines stare grimly ahead, indifferent to the big sweep of sand and rock that surrounds them.

The owl passes and this time I can almost feel it brush my face.

She stayed in town. I answer the phone late one night and the voice is there, giggling, husky, a ball of words bouncing down its own line of thought. She tells me she is a Christian now, Jesus Christ has become her Lord and Savior and this fact, she says, has helped a great deal. Could we get together? I say of course, but never call back. One day I am driving—I have just finished building a dome with Jake or, perhaps, I am heavily into honeybees. My old truck is acting up and the big black dog resents the desert summers. A local fungus expresses itself as Valley Fever and this is killing him. I pass an intersection and glance over at a woman waiting for the bus. She is fat and dressed mostly in black and she does not look adjusted to her weight, more like a small doll that has been inflated with a bicycle pump. It is Susan.

These moments fall behind me. I am on vacation in one of the little mountain ranges of southern Arizona, between marriages, and the woman feels a country inn with bed and breakfast would be just the tonic for our relationship. The big white clapboard building rambles and the yard of old trees promises shade. Across the way is a general store complete with pool table. We walk over and shoot a few games, sip beer and peer out the flyspecked windows at the railroad tracks. The old inn itself is a nightmare of quaint, the small rooms stuffed with furniture cursed at the moment of its conception in the late nineteenth century. Tiny bathrooms are shoehorned into former closets.

The cook is wrinkled, profane, loud, and deeply addicted to

a parody of the Old West. She appears to think she is a chuck wagon chef on some long ago cattle drive and mixes imperious commands with efforts at salty talk. The guests worship her rusticity as she plunks down a platter overflowing with thick steaks and continues the story of her bad marriages to bad men.

We flee the next morning and a soft rain falls on the playa near Willcox. Sandhill cranes stand guard over the flat, shallow puddle. I race the car toward the small community in the hope of finding a silent plate of ham and eggs. I feel the railroad tracks thump under my wheels and slow down as we enter the old center of the cow town. Empty storefronts line the street like death's-heads. I have the radio on, a broadcast from Tucson. The music ends and here comes the news.

The trained voice speaks in bursts of words and a small item catches my ear. There has been a fire at a home. The woman, according to police and fire department reports, pushed a dresser against the door, then poured some fuel around and set the bedroom ablaze. The woman is dead. They can give no name at this moment, something about notifying the family.

I know it is Susan. Well, she made it to her early thirties.

I drive north, drive very fast and the rain shifts more toward the raw force of a storm. The big mountains are swallowed and the desert glows with new colors. I pull into a motel and buy a bottle of champagne to restore a holiday spirit. We drink from clear plastic glasses. The cable television flickers messages from around the nation and late at night I watch a senator giving thoughtful answers to esoteric economic questions that have never occurred to me. The woman sleeps in the bed next to me, and she knows there is not much for her to say right now.

At dawn I take a walk and the big mountain, a rock pile of 10,000 feet, marks time within the black fist of the storm. *I was not there for her. This was not my job.* The rituals of guilt roll through my mind.

I remember her lips, the black hair, and I hear the laugh. We are walking down the hall of a college building, she holds a re-cord album cover before her and gives a small oration on the bulge in the lead singer's britches. We have left Latin class. I feel an unease at her fascination with the man's trousers, but we have left Latin class for good. I quickly wall off the past and look up at the mountain.

Susan is so easy to dismiss. There is the matter of the drugs, the sexual promiscuity, the failure to nail down that job at the five-and-dime, the inattention to regular hours, sound diet, cur-rent events, and Junior League. There is a factory somewhere off in heartland where they are manufacturing a chart—the coated, pull-down kind that high school teachers use to dazzle the inmates—and this one displays UnAmericanism, all the ticks and warps and vices and sins that prevent a human being from putting a hard shoulder to the GNP and joining the march of history. I look up at the chart and it is Susan. Notice the short skirt, no bra, sensuous use of makeup, hungry eyes, cigarettes stuffed carelessly in the purse. The schematic opens her head and finds no clear ideas, just fierce needs and demands. The vo-cabulary is profane, the nails long, red and sharp. The appetites are monstrous, as endless and frightening as the big lonely of the American landscape. The teacher speaks in a smug, controlled voice, the pointer dancing easily from disreputable feature to disreputable feature. I listen keenly. I am falling in love again.

The rain slaps my face and the mountain continues to sulk inside a fury of clouds. Back in the motel room the woman no doubt continues to slumber. The television, sound off, continues to flicker. Perhaps, we will marry. I can see the dining room table, the fine china, the complicated dishes deduced from the formulas of French texts, the repartee of amusing table talk. We will marry and drink fine wines and search for vintage years. In Susan's room, the odor must still linger, the raw force of the smoke, perhaps the stench of burning flesh. Surely, at this very moment long sheets of records snore in some psychiatrist's office where a careful hand has jotted down words that catch her hunger in the lingo of pathology and then the hand scribbles out the prescription for the appropriate drug that will make her view of the world vanish from her mind. Sometimes when things got a little rough, Susan would smash a shop window, create some little incident, to get her dosage made more generous. I can hear her laughter as she tells me of such tactics. I think of betrayal. I will go back to the motel room, where the future unfolds with calm and reason and order. I can't betray Susan. It is not possible. There is only me now.

I feel light rain against my face and wonder at the heat of a burning bed.

I lean against the block wall, drink bad water, and watch toilet paper blow in the wind. The parked trucks idle nearby and I can hear happy voices from the cafe kitchen. A mile to the north, the American line knifes across the hard desert. I drink bottle after bottle of water and nothing comes out, not for hours, six hours to be exact. I am down, far down. The temperature idles around 110. This is not going to work.

A scrap of toilet paper waves white petals among the creosote, skips along the ground and comes to rest on the thorns of a cholla. There are restrooms inside but many do not use them. The area behind the buildings is a mine field of human feces and blowing tissue. There is broken glass everywhere and lots of shiny and empty potato chip bags staring up from the dirt with bright eyes. Mexicans should not be eating potato chips . . . it ruins the local color. But they refuse to obey and America seems everywhere now.

This trip starts two nights ago. We stagger through the hot blackness and stumble in the fields along the Rio Sonoyta. The moon is new and gives very little help. We pass many huts, the families sleeping on old beds in the yard, dogs barking and snapping at our heels. There are no lights, none at all. Many of the fields hold rows of prickly pear cactus, the pads whacked off here and there. The Mexicans eat them as a salad. Brand new irrigation pumps sit like lords and stacks of unconnected pipe wait for more earth to make wet and soggy. When I was a boy I would see pumps in the desert running night and day. I have never trusted the pumps. They reach into the dark places of the earth, places blacker and more lonely than the grave. In the past decade, the cropland around Sonoyta has increased fivefold.

Bill and I say nothing about the pumps and pipes and thorny row crop of cactus. It will all fail. It always does. The water table will sink, the soil will grow white with salts, the peasants will get gloomy about their prospects and flee. For a hundred miles along the line this northern edge of Sonora is littered with such failures.

Then the desert will return. It is sleeping now beneath this field as I stumble in the darkness on the furrowed ground. It will wake up—you can count on this—and make the women old and wrinkled, the men crazy with heat and defeat, the crops writhe with pain as the cells in the leaves scream for rain and the roots shudder at the touch of the salts. Experts will be consulted, recommend various schemes, and then fail. They will not admit this failure. They never do. They prefer to tackle problems, endless problems, and call this work projects. I no longer have much to say about such matters. They seem necessary to my civilization. The desert must be attacked. And it is.

The heat is very heavy now, many tons on our shoulders, and we feel sick. That is the goal. We dream of 140 miles of heat, say 110 to 125 degrees in the shade. We will not die. Other people die. We will taste how these people die and that sensation will make life better for us. I lack Susan's willingness to leave. I think of her from time to time: I think, now she knows. I cannot accept fire. I will toy with thirst and heat. Sometimes I hear Susan screaming.

Sometimes I do not hear her screaming at all. Instead I see her sitting calmly on the bed and the flames are licking with bright orange tongues.

We walk for hours and see no snakes. We feel worse and worse as the heat moves deeper into our bodies. I lose my hat in the darkness. I will not notice this loss until dawn. Finally, we throw our packs off and sprawl on the ground against a little hill. The river bottom spreads before us, all blackness, the air rich with scents, the kind of air that invades the mouth and nose like gauze. We do not speak. We are very tired and can hardly eat, the candy bars stall in our throats and the work of chewing and grinding them becomes a repellent task.

My legs are bleeding. They always do. I can't seem to walk around things—that must be it since Bill almost never slashes his legs. I crash right through the brush, the thorny branches, and little streams of blood roll down my legs and etch warm, sticky sentences. When people first hike with me they sometimes ask why I walk through things. Often they laugh at me for scraping against the clumps of mesquite, ironwood, palo verde, catsclaw, and acacia. But at least they stop asking me why. I am grateful for this politeness because I have no answer.

Suddenly the darkness is punctured by voices and I stare down below and make out a hut. The family sits in the yard on little chairs. There is no fire, no lamp. They begin to sing, I cannot understand the words, and the sounds rise and flow across the desert night. Children break in, small laughs and giggles, the deeper voice of a man, the pure clarity of the woman. We listen for half an hour or more. The concert is very beautiful but the black night greedily devours it. The air is much too heavy for the additional burden of song and the family can hardly penetrate beyond their yard. Sweat rolls down my forehead. The woman sings of soap, clean sheets, of her man groomed and climbing on her in the hot night. The springs will creak and by first light the rose will be in bloom by the door. The lyrics are unmistakable even though I cannot make out the words.

THE CONCRETE BLOCKS feel hot against my back and I drink liter after liter of water. I am in shorts, I have a pack, and I wear running shoes. The Mexican guys hanging out at the gas station-garage-cafe cast glances at me and make jokes. I am not a man: I walk by choice. I stand and decide to move. The heat is wonderful, a complete and finished thing. I walk into the cafe and examine the glass case full of knickknacks for the traveler. A hat, a nice baseball cap, catches my eye and I buy one that says SAN FRANCISCO '49ERS. I order a Coca-Cola and hope the caffeine will fire up my kidneys. My system has clearly shut down.

A satellite photo hangs on the wall of the lower Colorado River and all the deserts clustered around it. I walk over and study it while the men in the cafe bore deep into my back. Once everything in the satellite image was a god, every square foot. Now all these spirits have been slain, buried in a mass grave and largely forgotten. For the early human beings the entire landscape was a raucous kind of temple; for my kind the entire landscape is real estate.

I am a lover of dead gods. I peer into the slick glossy image and catch a glimpse of the dance ground, the mesquite moon overhead, dust rising from our feet, my skin inscribed with bright lines of color, mysterious words pouring from my mouth, a pinch of corn pollen, the flutter of an eagle's feather. This is a pure fantasy. I can yearn but I cannot act. My mind has been rewired and the gods are gone. I will never believe in them, not for a single day. But still I yearn. The dead gods are said to have talked through animals and rocks and storms and sky and to have taught one how to join with the earth as surely as a man and woman dissolve into each other in the act of love.

I consider my situation. I cannot stand in front of the glossy satellite image forever. I sit down in a chair again and rest my arms on the formica tabletop. Bill has not yet arrived. He is still out there in the heat and thirst. He is in no danger. He is walking along the paved highway now. But he is surely hurting. The thing is too hard and we are too sick. I will wait right here, I decide. I drink Coke in the big room of the Mexican cafe, a fly lands and walks along my finger. I order a cup of coffee and the men at the other tables let their gaze drift off me and they return to talk of bad tires, frozen transmissions, and women they have loved and left but will love again. The cook is at my table now, and asks if I am hungry.

Yes, very hungry, but I cannot eat. I say, no thank you, and he smiles and pours me another coffee. He tells me it is very hot and I agree. The fly buzzes around the room.

I will wait for Bill. This god business is awkward, I lack the capacity for really discussing it. And yet, I sense something out there in the trail shrines, the secret caves, the prayer sticks, the animal shapes outlined on the desert floor by dead men as messages to dead gods.

Once I was working on a federal contract, a water and energy study, and I drove for a day to the north until I reached a canyon called Chaco. The canyon was full of ruins, big stone ruins, that told me clearly the dead people and their dead gods once lived here. I drove recklessly in a rented car and at one point on the washboard road, the rear window popped out of its rubber gasket and fell on the ground. I pitched it in the back seat. At the campground, I picked a place off from other visitors. I had a bag of marijuana, a case of beer, an ice chest full of steaks, and whiskey.

The wind blew all the time and there were warnings posted in the restrooms about the local menace from bubonic plague. The water was very alkaline and within half a day my bowels were loose and stayed that way. This happened to everyone at Chaco. The study I was to do called for the detailed examination of numbers, scientific papers, and a vast literature of technical lore.

I wanted something else. For days I walked the canyon and crawled through the ruins. The sun was warm, the dust and wind relentless. My steaks tasted like dirt. Nothing came to me but numbers, the tidy rows of charts, graphs and tables.

One day when the place was all but deserted—I think maybe the wind drove everyone else away—I visited a huge kiva. I sat in the middle and took off my clothes. I had a big corncob pipe and I packed it firmly with grass. The kiva was round, the stone work very carefully done. I sat for hours, alone in a swirl of marijuana. Nothing happened, nothing at all. But I saw convincingly that numbers would not be enough. I decided to put the land and the people, the living people and the dead people, into the study. I did this and turned in the report. I was fired.

I am on my third cup of coffee in the cafe and I am certain we will never finish this one. We are too weak, much too weak, and the heat is too strong. I walked into this cafe around noon, hatless and out of water. My lips were cracking and the pain was beginning in the muscles, the deep pain when the cells mutiny and demand fluid. My thoughts were scattering in the hot breeze and I could feel the heat of the earth boiling up through the soles of my running shoes. My stride was still sure and confident but there were ninety miles left to do and the sun said no, absolutely no, you are not ready. You are not clean.

I will never be clean. I know this now. I am not cut out for cleanliness. The machines are too seductive. I have only one real asset: I am willing. And that is not enough, not this time.

I drain my cup of coffee and slowly rise from the chair. I go outside into the heat. The block wall has not moved and I return to my position leaning against it. To the north, I hear the rumble of American jets as military exercises flood the sky just across the border. I imagine the pilots flashing above the desert floor, fingers ready on the trigger, mountains flaming past and the light a white blindness punching through the canopies. Every few minutes a big boom reverberates as the sound barrier falls before the genius of human beings.

You can do anything you wish here, for a while. That is part of the draw of deserts. Plant cities full of lakes and swimming pools, unroll golf courses like carpets. Always there is talk of new cities. People move and alter cities as a matter of course. I have seen women walk naked through the cactus and brush, sun sparkling on the thorns, and beads of sweat rolling down the curves of soft flesh. The sense of power and immunity is addictive. You can do anything you wish here, for a while.

That is the promise.

But night follows day. My body grows keen with the approach of this night. I smell its presence even in the white light of noon. In this night, everything fails—cities, kivas, wooly mammoths, mines, dire wolves, farms, giant sloths, spas. Of course, failure is part of the texture of the planet and the ultimate result of all efforts. It is easy to dismiss and even easier to miss.

But I think something must be said for the force of failure here. In the desert, failure has unmistakable force. Very little blocks the view. Bones strewn across the sand. Spent rockets gleaming against dull earth. Lonely graves. I was walking once, a very long walk of more than one hundred miles, and then I came upon a perfectly round rock, miles from a river. I was working up the valley more than thirty miles long, the land steady with creosote, perfectly spaced and total in its control. The rock was sitting all alone, and I stopped and reached down. My fingers rubbed along the worked edges where someone centuries before had ground out the shape and the round rock resting in my hand suddenly became a stone ball. A deliberate thing. But the players were gone, vanished.

Then there are the car bodies with flat tires and no key in the ignition. The mammoth bones poking out from the dirt bank, the corpses of drug dealers surfacing in the arroyos after a hard summer rain. Once in a great while a missing airplane returns to consciousness when some hiker stumbles upon the bent wings and the light, dry skulls.

It's not so easy to ignore the past here. Failure has force. The Indians are a problem also. They were not killed promptly and still retain ancestral lands. And they talk. The beasts too refuse to remain silent and discreet. I once stood next to a man's house at night not far from where his swimming pool squatted like a blue eye amid a grotto of fake rocks. The man pointed at the ground and showed me the exact spot where he found the track of a lion. I drive past houses where I once hunted deer. I sit by petroglyphs of bighorn sheep while fighter planes roar overhead at 100 feet and the stone shakes, but never blinks.

You can do anything you wish here, for a while.

SOMETIMES I DREAM of the ice. It is at moments like this, sitting against a hot wall in a hot desert, with trucks rumbling at idle next to the sticky asphalt and everyone wearing watches and synthetic fibers. This is when the thought of the ice comes. I want it all to end, the traffic to stop, the cities to fall away, the sound to die before the relentless wind. History will break—a stick snapped over my knee. Or perhaps, history as a big cable severed by giant shears. All the ideas, plans, hopes, and drives dangle helplessly from the end of the severed cable, useless wires empty of energy. There is that quick movement and then cries, screams, moanings, and then at last the silence falls.

That is the quality of the ice dream. It is a blue wall pushing across the land. The mountains are ground to powder, the cities and machines disappear beneath the forward march of the ice. Animals flee, plants go down, but the ice rolls on and there is no escape. The slate is swept clean for new beginnings. The radio empties even of static. There is a purity to this dream. Like a nuclear war, it is so total in its destructiveness that I am absolved from any act of intervention.

I do not dream often and hardly ever remember what I dream. So the ice seldom visits me. I do not like tidy things, so the ice seldom appeals to me. I am designed for only one place, exactly where I am with my back leaning against the wall in the 110-degree heat and my mind drifting across the desert and the splotches of sky.

I stare into the ice and see a wooly mammoth, the tusks curving in a state of grace. I reach forward and touch the hide. The hair is coarse, the skin wrinkled, the eyes focused on something I cannot detect. I smell my fingers and a mustiness pours into my nostrils. I step back and then to the side as the wall of ice grinds on, the mammoth riding carelessly at the front.

At other times I think the ice is not a dream. It is here and it is now. The ice is the age. I listen: there is an incredible screeching of metal on metal, the saguaros fall down, rocks explode, the light leaves the lion's eye and a fly lands on the dead lens. The deer becomes pulp between pile drivers. The tear of flesh, crack of bone, marrow oozing. Blood falls like drool down the lips of the machine.

I look up from my spot next to the block wall and the machine rolls patiently toward me, a vast hurly-burly of gears, rollers, belts, sieves, bins, grinding stones, blades and drains. The desert disappears into this contraption. I get up and step to the side of the lumbering behemoth, then shift and see behind the mechanism a long carpet of homes, offices, roads, parking places, power plants, electric lights, garbage trucks, and squad after squad of mail carriers stuffing envelopes into numbered slots. People move across this carpet, well dressed, the women snug in bright fabrics. The sound of the machinery is deafening to me, but the people in the carpet seem oblivious to the thunder. I step forward, bounce lightly off the hot desert soil and onto a street. There is a cafe, the sign hand-painted on a board, a delicate flower smiling in one corner. I slip through the door. The walls glow with big posters of trees, cactus, bighorn sheep, rabbits nibbling succulent leaves—the green of those leaves is almost unbearable. A handwritten menu lies on the well-varnished table. I glance over lists of homemade pies, omelets fat with avocados, onions and cheeses. The tea is herbal, the beers imported and today the special is a curry. The men wear cotton shirts, the women shun bright makeup and favor many bracelets. No one speaks loudly, ferns sway in ceiling baskets. The silverware is solid and feels good in my hand.

I am at home here.... I am at ease. I am truly in the grip of the ice. The waitress takes my order. This time the ice does not come from the north, a carpenter's plane shaving down the land. This time it comes from within me.

I drain another canteen of water. The heat is steady, the flies lazy. I go back into the cafe. Perhaps coffee is the key. The sun falls through the doorway and pounds the floor. I can feel the cement slab shudder under the force. I sit. I wait.

Bill straggles in, his face a tapestry of fatigue. The trip is ending and we will spend a few restless hours before admitting this fact. We hardly speak, and he joins me in pouring fluids down as rapidly as possible. The cook smiles but Bill cannot face food.

I sit in the cafe sipping strong coffee while for hundreds and thousands of square miles around me the land is empty of residents but dense with the clutter of human dreams. All along the wire, wetbacks are marching north toward those jobs, drug smugglers are attending to the important details of their craft, supersonic aircraft are needling the sky chasing the forward edge of time.

Bill and I go outside to continue our guzzling of water in the shade of the wall. Ants troop across the ground and make periodic ascents on our limbs. We do not care. We are too spent to defend borders. The sky begins to clot with clouds. It is late summer and the monsoon teases the desert with hints of rain.

The clouds pack together and then go black. A rain begins to fall to the north, the sun is bright against the drops, and the tower of water swings to and fro across the cactus like a tornado. The wind comes up and blows dust in our eyes.

We cross the highway and go back into the malpais to visit an old man. The men in the cafe call him Don Francisco. He lives in a tin shack with no windows and his door opens to a big ramada supported by mesquite posts. His job entails guarding a two-track road that leads to a cinder mine and secret airfield. We approach his hut, pause and politely wait, and the old man comes out. He is in his sixties, hair gray but full, skin brown, body still firm and erect. He smiles. His little dog dances around our feet.

The old man quickly pulls up two folding chairs, the legs bent with use, and motions us to sit. A wood fire smokes in the corner of the ramada and water heats for coffee. Don Francisco is a man of the world. His wife works as a domestic in Los Angeles, and his son is a chauffeur in San Francisco. He stays in the desert with his dog. The house has no electricity, no stove, no air conditioner, no toilet, no space. The walls enclose maybe ten feet by ten feet.

Bill palavers with the old man in the ritual courtesies of Spanish and we sit there and talk, flies swirling around our faces. Time creeps along and the desert is fresh with scents kicked up by the rain and to the west the wall of the dunes rises golden in the fading light. Don Francisco insists that we sleep under his ramada but this I do not want to do. I do not like roofs. I try to explain this but he will have none of my excuses until suddenly I tell him I must see the stars, *las estrellas,* and he nods and smiles.

We sleep that night on a clearing of black stones just south of his shack. The heat has weakened after the rain but the air is heavy with moisture and presses against our bodies. Tomorrow we will either get up and walk the hundred miles to Yuma or we will get up and thumb a ride eighty miles to the next border crossing. It hardly matters. In the night, I rise and stagger from my nest on the ground. The lights of the machines sweep down the highway and around the cafe I hear human voices laughing. To the south there is only blackness. The airfields are quiet now ... the harvest of marijuana will not begin for a month or so. I can make out the peak of Pinacate in the faint moonlight and stars fill the sky. I am barefoot and the stones dig into the soles of my feet. My body aches.

I am slow.

This is the key American landscape of my time. In the nineteenth century, the Rocky Mountains triggered words like awesome and sublime—the meadows lush with rich light and comforting green, the alpine forests cluttered and safe, the rock spires sketching one face of God. That was the terrain of a nation lunging toward empire, conquest, genocide and violent seizure of the land. It was the fantasy land of a Republic that slaughtered a half million of its citizens in a Civil War, the optic drug that helped ease the horror of Wounded Knee. It was an image that was packed with Victorian knickknacks for the eye: the horizon is never endless, it is just high and huge.

The desert has now seized this part of the American mind. The United States is a sell, and the sellers, the advertisers, use the Mojave, the Sonoran desert, the rock of the Colorado Plateau, the hard flats of the Great Basin for their pitch. This cannot be an accident. They sense what our souls crave. And these are very different lands for the imagination to wander.

Cheap postcards and expensively designed business logos

push forth saguaros as the emblems of the wild, free ground. The cactus, the sandy wastes now appear as the arena where Americans can still dream America. This hardly means that we have reached some new harmony with the deserts. The deserts of the Southwest are being destroyed by fast-growing populations, by roads knifing into back country, by bulldozers toppling giant cactus for subdivisions, by smog sinking the air, by wells draining the aquifers, dams choking the rivers. But as the land dies, and it is dying, the mind, our minds, pump more and more power into the surviving landscape. The deserts speak to some deep need in modern people, and with luck, they will teach us some ideas long discarded in our recent and continuing orgy of machines, booming cities and vast hordes of personal property. These ideas will bring scant comfort.

The new desert people, the city inhabitants of the region, will be locked in urban enclaves for the rest of their lives. They will live in dense, dirty communities, work at desks, fill out forms, learn the languages of computers, not that of owls or wolves. And from time to time they will look out their sealed windows or walk through a patch of cactus and creosote and be flooded with doubts about the security of their worlds. Then they will hear the deserts talk.

The hard lands are not just another place. Here human ambitions are instantly diminished. Everywhere one looks the ground shouts mortality, rupture, unevenness. The deserts are like an X-ray: everything in them reveals its bones. The mountains mock the skyscrapers. The shortest walk suggests the body will surely die, rot and sink into the earth. The space dwarfs notions of conquest, and the heat flattens desire.

Time is endless here. The sierras speak millions and billions of years. The native American communities utter hundreds and thousands. These are not just numbers in the books. The life of a man or woman is nothing against this ocean of time. You must quickly pull the drapes shut, you must block that view of the desert outside, and block it now.

There is something brooding about the space that destroys the borders of the identity. When I visit the plains, walk the grasslands and become a dot in the sea of green, I always feel alone, separate, acutely aware of myself in the bland miles of grass waving in the wind. The terrain does not obliterate my sense of self, it makes it more severe. The deserts are different. Here the individual, after a good while and with some luck, melts into the land. You lose an exact sense of where your body ends and the trees, cactus, mountains, bajadas, and flats begin. I have a hunch it is this feeling that has triggered all the mystics, hermits, mad hatters, prophets and messiahs that have issued from the deserts of this world—the mad men and mad women filing strange reports of talks with God and the devil.

The deserts force us to think rather than argue. I sense a new way of thinking emerging from the contact made in this century between the modern Americans and the ancient ground surrounding them. On the face of it, such a change in thinking would appear unlikely. The recent boom in the desert is not the kind one expects to produce a bumper crop of insights. It is crass, bustling, vulgar, cheap, ugly and has the soul of a real-estate swindler. But ideas tend to come from grubby places.

I will bet my life on this place. The emptiness will tell us what we need to know. Whether we listen or not.

I AWAKEN AT first light and stare out at the oven warming up for the day. We are truly finished. We hurt. We are sick with heat. To the north, the jets begin their morning roar as the war games continue in the United States. I walk over to the cafe and have a cup of coffee. Bill and I say little. We are leaving. We have been defeated and we do not like the ring of that word.

In a few minutes we hitch a ride west on the back of an old flatbed. The machine strains up the hills and every so often we must pull over and let the engine cool. The Mexicans driving the truck take these pauses in good spirits. The ride itself takes a long time and the sun cooks us well. At the border crossing, we hitch another ride north. The man driving is a wetback and wants us to assure him we are not La Migra. He is a happy man with a home in Yuma, Arizona, and a second place to stay in San Luis, Sonora. The border, the fences, the laws, are a pesky swarm of gnats surrounding his life but he has grown adjusted to these annoyances.

He drops us at a bus station, I buy a biography of the Kennedy family and read of dreams of dynasty in air-conditioned comfort as the desert flits past, a harmless mural coating my window.

I am back after thirty years, once again walking down the rows of kin in the burying ground of Germantown, Iowa. The stone slabs whisper Beermann, Stoeckmann, Meyer, Richter, Dobertin and on and on, a flutter of voices flooding the afternoon air with German prayers and sayings and pleas toward God that I no longer can decipher. The grass is neatly cut and this tidiness makes me uneasy. Then the lines of corpses end and the fields begin, steady, regular rows of soybeans and corn that race outward and claw at the horizon. The dead outnumber the living in this hamlet of sixty-five and the Lutheran church towers over everything, its white spike shafting the sky for more than a century.

Everybody buried in the cemetery is my kin. Everybody for miles around is tied to me by half-forgotten marriages, births, love affairs, moody swirlings of blood. Like many American families, my people have flourished and there are teams of aunts and uncles and dozens of cousins and the children of cousins. Some have prospered, some have not. Some have gone to college, some to jail. And now I am the descendant come home from the fleshpots of the West.

Five hours ago I was in the Sonoran desert with the heat, the Sunbelt boom beating against my body as I dragged my bags across the parking lot to the Phoenix airport. I saw new glass walls flaring in the morning light and I could smell money in the breeze. The city cowered under a lid of bad gases as the free-way rumbled with rush-hour traffic. In the terminal everyone beamed with energy, the flesh carefully tanned, the clothing some mixture of California sportswear, Stetsons and boots. The women were very trim, the pants tight, the faces well lacquered against the intruding eyes of strangers. And all the people present a mix of emotions I can never really prove but always sense in this new land dubbed Sunbelt: They are defiantly confident and yet morose.

Like many modern Westerners, I am torn between two worlds, almost two distinct bloods. My early years are rooted in wetter, older, more settled terrain—in my case the Midwest—but my present and future are bound to the raw, ugly energy of the instant cities, to the endless miles of plain buildings that now dot a region once written off as a backwater hellhole. Many object to the ferocity of life in the Southwest but few can deny the pull of all that energy. When I go back to the used-up, crowded Midwest, the old sensations return and I anticipate a feeling much like sleep, a deep, soothing sleep.

I feel the raw, cool wind whipping across the graves and try to imagine myself sinking back into the legendary American bedrock, the family farm with the white chickens scratching in the yard, the apple pie cooling on the window sill, the good earth under my feet and the safe, sure beliefs drenching the air. This is half of my genetic code, my mother's people, sturdy krauts dreaming big harvests and fighting weird theological wars with other synods of Lutherans.

There were trees everywhere when I glanced out the plane window at the meandering Missouri River and the humid air seemed to have the weight of a lead sheet. Everyone in the

Omaha terminal was pale and well-fleshed and not ashamed to devour a couple of pork chops for breakfast. I noticed one thin blonde with long hair, the skin a parchment. The return seemed so easy at first but after an hour or two of driving the small state highways, the trail back faded and I was suddenly a stranger in a strange country. Farms murmured unexpected messages as my car sped past. WAR IS OBSOLETE offered one hand-painted sign in a barnyard. Twenty minutes later I spotted a wooden sign nailed to a tree by an abandoned farmhouse: SOLD OUT. Ah, I thought, all those problems I heard about between the songs on FarmAid.

After a hundred miles, I realized I had seen no chickens in the farmyards and no gardens beside the neat houses. Big machines rested on enormous and perfect lawns, but I saw no people out about the barns and no one working in the fields. The dull eyes of satellite dishes stared up toward the blue sky and a steady wind whipped across the prairie. And then I pulled over, got out and walked through the small gate. I stand in the burying ground hoping the dead people will help me conjure up a lost world.

I drive a half mile into the village center and walk into Lloyd's, Germantown's only saloon. My great-grandmother's house is across the road. When I was child, she lived in the white frame building alone and rode out her nineties, doing her own ironing, sputtering out messages in a German I could not understand and staring at me through her fading eyes—probably wondering about this small stranger her blood had finally thrown up. She was very limber and her face looked like corrugated cardboard. The house smelled of years, solitude and the astringent chemicals of age. There were tales about her. After her first husband died, she would stand before her bedroom window and look out across the orchard to the burying ground. Her children thought their mother was grieving for her dead man. Then one evening they discovered a townsman scaling a ladder up to that second story bedroom—my great-grandmother had been signaling him in the orchard where he waited. The children forced a marriage. In later years a couple of sheep prowled the yard as her lawn-mowers—waste not want not—and helped fertilize the lush, green expanse. They are gone now, the house remodeled with new siding and additions. The white picket fence has vanished, and Grandma is sleeping out in the burying ground.

A poster of martial arts star Chuck Norris glares from the saloon wall and across the room the only customer, an old man who introduces himself as Wilbert, sits on a stool sipping a beer. Small talk passes between us and he politely investigates who I am and then, when I give a few clues, quickly rifles his mind and correctly places me in the local genealogy. "Ah, Berdina's boy," he says with satisfaction. "Why we were children together, you tell her to come see me next time she is in Germantown." I feel like Alex Haley doing his roots thing up some African river.

A small xeroxed sheet is taped to the mirror of the back bar:

STRESS
That confusion created when one's mind overrides the body's basic desire to choke the living shit out of some asshole who desperately needs it.

I nod toward the sign and the lady tending bar looks up and starts explaining to me that a Germantown woman mailed it back from her new home—Phoenix, Arizona—where she sells real estate. Then there is the Germantown woman who is working as a CPA in Tucson, the local man living in Mesa, and suddenly Wilbert chimes in at the mention of Mesa and says, "By golly, that Mesa. Why a lot of the local farmers go there in the winter. Boy is it a going place. They all head out there when the crops are in." The barkeep herself has just returned from Phoenix—the thunderstorms! my heavens!—where she attended an insurance convention with her husband—was it hot!—and the monsoon rains poured down every day.

The room is dark and there is a hint of betrayal in the air and yet all I hear is talk of the Sunbelt, the boom, the sunny winter months under a desert sky. I plunge ahead.

How about the crops?

"The crops? Oh, they look good," the barkeep says in a flat voice. "The beans are good, the corn is good and nobody is sure what they will do with the crop. There is no space left to store it and the price is bad, less than what it costs to plow, plant and harvest."

I feel suddenly at ease, I am back in my childhood during the fifties when farmers always sat around bewailing their costs, denouncing the government, and bemoaning the price they got for their crops. She spins on to paint a portrait of granaries overflowing on the farms, machine sheds being converted to crop storage, corn being piled up in the open air on Midwest main streets, of federal bins with waiting lists, of a gusher of corn, a glut, a rich outpouring from the fecundity of the dark black soil. The notes are falling due at the banks, the bills are going unpaid. The wolf is at the door, and so on.

And everyone goes to the Sunbelt. This is the strangest kind of economic ruin I have ever encountered, one based on $50,000 tractors, satellite-dish television and long winter vacations. Iowa has ninety-nine counties and seventy of them have lost people in the last five years—17,000 citizens booted off their farms and 50,000 people fleeing the state for good.

I sip my beer and sit on my stool amid the debris of the American family farm. My people broke the sod on the neighboring prairie, and all around me are their descendants in spotless houses with flowers in the yard and rooms so orderly that you feel like an intruder when you walk in and sit down. That is the overpowering memory of my childhood—the rigid, sterile rooms with linoleum so polished you could ice skate, the Prussian order in the knickknacks. And now they all know Phoenix, Tucson, "that Mesa," and the fishing along the Colorado River. There are no chickens and I see no Holsteins milling around the barns waiting to be milked. And when the crops come in, why everybody leaves because they can.

I am in the heart of the country and it is wrapped tight in the golden strands of the Sunbelt. I stand to leave, Wilbert comes over to shake my hand—half a finger is missing, the basic farmer wound from some encounter with a piece of machinery. He says, "Be sure and tell Berdina to stop by and see me. I'm out at my sister's place." He scribbles his name on a bar napkin.

WALLY TOOK ME fishing as a boy and we stood by the shore of Lake Shetek in southwestern Minnesota and the sky went black, boiling and swirling with anger. He peered up with his red farmer face and said, "Don't worry, those are wind clouds," and within minutes torrential rain fell. He wore bibbed overalls, worked leased land like a maniac from dawn to dusk, and when the harvest was ready, ran his combine far into the night, until the dew fell. Every now and then he went to town and drank too much. His whole world was northwestern Iowa and southwestern Minnesota and that was fine by him.

Once we had to haul a trailer from central Wisconsin back to Minnesota. He stood on the main street of La Crosse, along the Mississippi, watching the time and temperature flash on a bank sign and said over and over, "By golly, what won't they think of next," and that was the big trip of a decade for Wally. Sometimes when the farm work fell into one of those seasonal stalls that occur between bouts of plowing, planting, cultivating and harvesting, he would drive miles to my aunt's place, play pinochle until the small hours of the morning and then go back to his work with a smile.

He spent World War II in the Pacific and when he got discharged in Los Angeles, he bought, borrowed or begged an automobile, drove off and rolled and rolled across the country, drove day and night, and he never stopped rolling until he got home to Minnesota. Then he stayed put. He was home.

I HAVE BEEN here twenty-four hours and I have not seen a fox, a pheasant, a bird on a wire, a hawk, or a rabbit, and but one chicken. I dismiss this observation. I am hardly a naturalist. But this sense of something missing gnaws at me and I park my Hertz car near a government-preserved marsh, walk, find a deer track and then the handprint of a raccoon in the mud. Three Canadian geese—a species recently restored to the area—honk overhead, a goldfinch darts into some brush, and I am a boy again, dreaming of sighting down on a big buck. I turn and go up a low hill and then suddenly the fields begin again and the straight rows knife across a void that is empty of everything but corn, soybeans, and poisons to control the unruly yearnings of the earth.

The absence of hawks disturbs me. I try to remember if they were present when I was a boy and my mind says yes, yes, and I catch the silhouette flickering on the edge of memory, the hulking shape on the telephone pole studying the land for flesh, the shadow in the barnyard terrifying the chickens. I sense their presence and power in the abandoned corridors of my mind. In Arizona they are everywhere, staring off the top of the saguaro, riding the thermals of summer with no doubt in their keen eyes. I have seen them coasting in the desert sky above the shopping malls, and talked with falconers as they sang about the merits of redtails and the menace of their talons. I have grown used to hawks. I have grown dependent on their existence for my sense of place. But they do not seem to be here in the green heart of the continent.

A dead shrew curls in the grass by my feet.

LAKE PARK, IOWA, is the other half of my DNA, the failed town of 900 where my father's people settled a century ago. Once in a while the community surges past 1000, but as my late Uncle Lum once told me, "Everytime a woman gets pregnant around here, a man leaves town." The sign coming in boasted 1100 people, but my aunt advises me that this number has shrunk by 200 in the past two years as sinking farm prices have settled on the town like permanent winter.

I drive past my grandfather's house, a small box the size of a hut but even so the home where he raised eight children, ran a still in the cellar, kept a few goats and sallied forth to the saloons on Main Street in his role as the local character and sometimes terror. When he'd come home drunk late at night he would bang on the door and holler at his wife, "Is the Widow Bowden home?" The women whisper he used to beat her. Now no Bowdens are home and there is a current Lincoln Continental parked in a new garage and the house has been restored and spruced up beyond all recognition.

I wander around the town cemetery with my cousin and find a grave marked CHARLES FREEMAN BOWDEN, a man I've never heard of, and my cousin says, "Oh, that's Free, grandpa's brother," and I envy any man known as Free. We finally find the family plot, rows of small stones with names and dates, the men's markers all carefully recording their military units in America's successive bursts of war.

I try and remember the world of men with red faces, the barnyards rich with the stench of livestock, the barbed wire tugging at my pants as I hopped the fence and picked up my .22 and continued hunting rabbits into the dusk. I feel the heft of a basket of fresh eggs, see again the ambitious rows of the gardens, taste the weak coffee and hear the talk salted with gosh darns, gollys, and I'll be damneds. And almost everything is gone, and a lot of it has gone to Arizona.

We drive out to another cousin's farm for a reunion. There is volleyball, beer, chairs out on the grass, whiskey, lots of photos of children, and talk, days of talk. My cousin Rich spent part of last winter fishing on the Colorado near Parker. My cousin Bill winters there each year. One cousin on welfare is talking about her upcoming vacation in Cancún. And cousin Bob wandered the Southwest last winter too. There is nothing to keep them home. I sit under the big trees by the farmhouse drinking beer with the men and there are no chickens, no geese, no ducks, no turkeys, no dairy herd. A few pigs and calves feed in the pens, but they seem mainly entertainment and most likely will be shipped to the Sioux Falls slaughterhouse when the time for the winter break beckons.

The fences all went down in the seventies when high crop prices enticed farmers to plow up every square inch of land. The wildlife left with the fences when the brush that had flourished beneath the strands of barbed wire vanished. The deer are booming but that is about it. I still have not seen a hawk.

Rich points out a big water tower to the south, a steel hulk planted in a cornfield that services not a town but the local farms. Their own wells can no longer be trusted. Nitrate poisoning, he explains, from all the fertilizer he and all my kin pour on the land. A baby died from nitrate water a week ago in the Dakotas, he continues, just turned blue and died.

A hell of a note, the men all agree, a hell of a note. But nothing stops the sprays, the nitrates, the endless fields. Last year the government chipped in $25 billion in price supports for the huge crops no one can use and no one can stop. The farm debt of Iowa now exceeds the national debt of Peru. A hell of a note.

I ask about the hawks, the big raptors that bewitched me as a boy when I wandered the fields with my .22, dreaming of bringing one down. The men seem puzzled by the question, as if I had just switched the conversation to latest novels written in Urdu.

"You're right," they allow, "now that you mention it, Chuck. There are hardly any hawks anymore."

"Do people shoot them," I ask impatiently. Christ, I seem to have returned here after decades as some kind of nature prig.

"Hell no," they snort. "They're protected by law. Anyway, who would bother? Nobody keeps chickens anymore, except for factory operations, and those birds never get outside the building they're kept in."

"What about mice?" I persist, "Are there lots of mice out in the fields?"

They hesitate and kind of look at me like I am even crazier than they had feared. I am a suspect creature at best, a man without real work, a scribbler, a person with untrimmed hair and God knows what habits—my one cousin calls me a hippie and I think, well, I wanted to return to the past.

"Well, no," they say. "There is not much out there but crops."

I swallow some more beer and hear a loud snap as the food chain breaks.

We amble down to the machine shed where my cousin shelters his harvesting machine—$60,000 new, but he picked it up for $15,000, probably at one of those fire sales that regularly occur now as locals give up the ghost and go bankrupt. The cab is air conditioned, the control panel as studded with dials as a jet plane's, and the doors boast simulated, hand-tooled leather. My brother's wife climbs up with my cousin and they go ripping around the farmyard, the huge machine lumbering like a beast from some forgotten age when wild things roamed the land.

I STAY IN a motel at the nearby town of Spirit Lake, a place the Sioux visited in 1857 while massacring some whites, thus putting Spirit Lake on the American map as a slight pause in the conversion of the prairie from wild ground into a food machine. Out my window is Lake Okoboji and the small body of water is ringed with fine homes and classy resorts.

The bar looks through a glass wall to the indoor pool and jacuzzi where pale people cavort in the water at 10 P.M. The cocktail waitress has startlingly blonde hair that is cropped short and spiked on top. The eyes stare blankly from a well of makeup, the face is passive, cool, and big city. The earrings dangle and when she moves they sway and gleam with gold. She wears black, everything black, and leans against the wall smoking a dark thin cigarette. The nails are long and very well cared for. She says she has not been to church in three weeks and she had better go tomorrow.

Outside, outside the resort walls where the cool night begins, there the endless fields sprawl, fields rolling restlessly over the hills and bottomlands, fields charged with the finest chemicals man can devise, lovingly contoured by the best equipment on earth, fields fierce in their green, earth rich and fertile, ground where the corn snaps in the night because it is so eager to grow and cast down seed, where the soybeans display perfect leaves, leaves no insect dare touch, leaves no rodents scurry under, a terrain engraved with rows innocent of foxes, huge pans of green that never reflect off a hawk's eye, there, outside the resort, all over the universe of Iowa a fertility rite is occurring, one midwifed by banks, machines, by chemists busy with their Bunsen burners and beakers of odd-colored fluids, a juicy, dripping ritual of fecundity that reverberates all around the planet, a musk of sex and procreation so powerful that it wafts across the long tables in the government cabinet rooms of Moscow, Washington, Paris, London, Tokyo, outside, outside, it is all out there, hidden in the darkness but still moving and evolving, the roots sucking nitrogen and moisture up, the leaves stirring, the corn struggling like a woman with a breech birth, and then going snap.

I do not ask the barmaid about Arizona because she will know. Now everyone knows. It is America's second home. For me, Arizona was once my Ultima Thule. The map of the United States in my Chicago elementary school offered huge swatches of color for the nation's various terrains … the greens of the east, midwest and south with their hardwood forests and irksome rains breeding rank growths; and further west in the places beyond my knowing, reds, all manner of reds, intense, dark reds, where the rains stopped, the mountains flared up, and men did not wear suits and ties and go to the office and where I imagined there were no tidy squares marked off by barbed wire, a place where there were no borders. At seven, eight, and nine, I was absolutely certain of this last point. When I was a child and my father announced to my uncle that we were moving to Arizona, my uncle roared, "How can you do that? How can you move to that Godforsaken, rattlesnake-infested hellhole? We'll never see you again."

I leave the bar and walk down the corridor. A woman stands before me with a bonnet on and a long calico dress. She is part of the cast of *Paint Your Wagon* and the show is now over in the resort. She cradles a plastic baby in her arms and looks fiercely ahead toward the American horizon where an EXIT sign glows red in the hotel night.

THE COWS WERE milked before first light and I would carry a warm, steaming bucket into the kitchen and plop it down by the sink and the hand pump. My aunt would begin mountains of pancakes, platters of thick bacon that did not curl, a yellow sea of scrambled eggs. Then to the hog house to feed the shoats, up in the barn tossing down hay to the stock, my child's hand reaching under the wary hen to pluck a warm egg, an amble through the orchard seeking the first ripe apple, a day spent hauling wagonloads in from the field, my sense of power soaring as I guided an old IH tractor. Finally the night falls, the heavy meal at the wooden table, sounds of a radio playing, games of cards, perhaps a burst from the hand-cranked phone on the wall, and then sleep, the breeze playing with the leaves in the grove.

Now I sit in an Iowa cafe, the comforting smell of coffee slapping my face awake, and I read in the newspaper that a new tractor stalks this landscape, a behemoth with 525 horsepower, the heft of 20 tons, and a price tag of $186,000, and the article states that on this machine a single man can plow 400 acres in eight hours. Decades ago, one of my uncles farmed 320 acres and that was considered a big farm, perhaps too big, but certainly all the land one man could decently care for.

I drive up the lane after thirty years of absence, my aunt dead, my uncle dead, and Skinner, an old codger, hanging on as the caretaker. I stand in the dining room and the place seems small now. The current owner is an absentee Nebraska doctor, my cousin as it happens. Skin hobbles around on his bad leg sputtering about his new tractor-style lawnmower. He drags me outside, fires it up and spins around the yard. Skin stumbled into a good thing years ago—this farm. He came up the lane broke and became the hired hand and then my uncle died and my aunt stayed on, my cousin bought the place, some local farmer with ambition—and probably a ton of debts—worked the land on lease, and Skin and my aunt settled into a decade-long card game at a few pennies per point.

I break away and go out to the barn. The building is empty of cattle, hay, cats and smell. Nothing but dust, air heavy with dust. The pens outside are down, the ground is now tilled right up to the buildings. There is no fallow ground, no meadows: the food machine. The hog house, the hen house, the granary are similar tombs empty even of cadavers. There is not a sound on the place. I walk off into the grove, the trees dying and tumbling down, and remember plugging my first crow. The birds have flown this place.

These weary farms do not have the feel of the new country that now claims me, the promised ground of the Sunbelt where at last all the dreams will come true. The Midwest is a charnel house. The Southwest is a financial obstetrics ward. I remember walking into a foothills saloon under the brooding stone of the Santa Catalinas. The energy rips across the room in waves. The bar is dark wood, flutelike music dripping from large speakers this afternoon, laughter and a parquet dance floor. A stained-glass outline of a bull and cow stares from the backbar mirror. He wears a dinner jacket, she holds a cigarette holder in her hoof. The room crackles with talk.

"I definitely want to hold to it for at least a year and see where that Broadway Corridor ends up. I want to walk away with at least forty or fifty made on the deal."

On the wall an oil painting of a load of steers scurrying from the chute of a holding pen—you can sense the slaughterhouse in their quick moves.

"Happily, everything will move the way he likes it to. He's a survivor."

"You can't beat that with a stick."

"The unions?"

"There may be some violence."

"There you go—jump back into reality."

There is a demanding hunger in the air as the promise of Saturday night approaches.

"Chicago is where I found out what taxis are all about. . . . And then we hit a traffic jam on the expressway. He didn't even say anything, he just pulled right off on the shoulder and drove ahead. That guy got a tip that day."

By the saloon door the faint afternoon light plays off a bronze of a cowboy on a bucking horse. I am mesmerized by the casual dreams of money. I cannot feel or sense any link between the talk in this room and the earth that supports all talk. The voices continue.

"Tucson is hurting for a real good club."

MY COUSINS' CHILDREN are scattered to both coasts, to the cities, the professions, steady checks, new cars, paved streets. Everywhere you go now it is the same America. Sonja is of the previous generation, the generation that stayed and tried to be the American farm. She sits over her breakfast and patiently struggles to explain the past to her sister's son. She is speaking of the early 1960s but the words sound much older. Her nephew is now a management consultant hustling a buck in New York. She talks of living on $1000 a year, never eating out, growing all your own food, sewing all your own clothes, putting up hundreds of jars of vegetables, jams, potted meats, of slaughtering your own hog or steer if you were going to eat pork or beef at all.

Her words do not register. The children have marched into a different country of silicon chips, apartments, credit cards, and cable television, and they call themselves dentists, geologists, speech pathologists—many things. The spawn of my mother's people and my father's people have scattered into the richness of America. One runs a machine shop in Chicago; another has green and blue hair and tends bar in a gay joint in San Francisco. They have become everything but farmers. When I was a boy, I dreamed, and my dreams were of being a farmer.

Back at the farm, the reunion winds down. We sit under the trees as night falls and let mosquitoes feed on us and we talk. Inside a card game fills the house with laughter and shouts. The kids get fed up with the slowness of it all and roar off into town to rent some movies for the VCR.

I PULL THE car off the road by a huge cornfield. Overhead a rough-legged hawk hovers in the air, apparently an early arrival from the summer ground of the Canadian Arctic. I whip out my binoculars and eye the bird and wonder what it kills and how the hunting goes in this machine-molded landscape of straight rows.

I feel awkward objecting to this fertile order, but I am filled with unease. It is this matter of hawks, I think, something about the hawks. We have won everything here and I am frightened by the completeness of our victory. The land is producing harvests that would have staggered my dead aunts and uncles and this bounty means that fewer people can make a living from the dangerously generous soil. Loneliness hangs over the fields. I gaze at some nearby acres where as a boy I worked on combining crews and baling crews. At noon the women would appear magically with platters of fried chicken, home-baked bread, mashed potatoes, sweet corn, black coffee, cakes and pies. We would sit on the ground and feast amid talk and laughter, everyone participating in a kind of annual commune and cooking contest.

That is gone now. Fences are down, fields are huge, machinery is mammoth, farms are much larger, farmers are few. The children have fled. There is a word now that everyone knows, a word no one ever spoke when I was a boy: Sunbelt. I am one of the many small dots in the census tables that have created the word. I stare into the corn and catch a glimpse of the huge human shuffle that has poured people into the deserts of the Southwest.

The hawk, my only hawk, continues to hover and slowly beat its wings against the wind. I am hypnotized by this simple act. There is no other sign of animal life until a clot of birds appears and mobs the raptor against the dull green horizon. Cars race by and then slow briefly, the drivers glance over at me staring up at something in the sky and I can tell by the way their eyes move and the way their lips form that they are wondering just what in the hell I could be looking at. Or for.

The woman sits on the single folding chair facing the empty desk in the bare room of the Mexican police station. The blue dress sets off her China eyes, the long black hair trails. The face is lovely, the skin smooth, the figure slender. She is desire in a building of denial. I want to ask her everything, but do not. Her hands relentlessly finger and crumple a small paper napkin.

I move swiftly past. The wooden staircase creaks and winds, paint sags off the walls. The man squatting in front of the head office means wait. The map of Nogales, Sonora, is taped up, a maze of *colonias* nestled in the hills with winding streets, arteries ending in stubs against steep slopes. To the east lies the Buenos Aires district, a bailiwick of drugs and homicide. The police show photographs of recent bodies found in the colonia, hands tied, faces skillfully slashed with knives, bullets propelled economically through the skulls. Within Buenos Aires' web of crooked streets is Río Hondo, the birthing ground of Ignacio Robles Valencia. The family home is small but boasts an indoor toilet. He is dead a few weeks and was called "El Nacho." I have come for his paper bones.

I am wary. The police station is the black hole where the laws end and there are never witnesses. A man about five-foot-three walks in with an AR-15 hanging idly in one hand, the other hand pushing a woman forward. The man at the desk asks, "Any trouble?" The man with the rifle shakes his head. The woman wears a red dress with black polka dots. She breathes rapidly and eyes the room with fear. It is three in the afternoon on a June day, and the air roasts at around one hundred degrees.

On the drive down to the line, a raven flaps over the truck, beak open, the specter panting in the white light. My eyes stare through the cracks of my windshield and sink into the bundle of feathers. I imagine the raven sharing no cares with the machines tracking the straight highway. And I feel envy.

I shove a tape into the player and hear Dylan's requiem for the sixties, "Señor (Tales of Yankee Power)." The words wrap around my head like a warm towel. I am crossing the line.

The Regis Saloon is hardwood backbar, Mexican men staring into their drinks, a bartender who hates cops, and a sign saying no one may enter with a gun or a uniform. The clink of the glasses being cleaned and stacked breaks through the noise of the television. "Nacho? El Nacho?" The bartender leans forward, the eyes cautious. "Yes, yes, I was raised with him in the colonia but it is not safe to speak of him." Why? He is dead, he is a corpse. "Yes, yes, but his family is not dead, his gang is not dead." He scurries away.

I think of Susan. She would have liked this place. Just down the street a mile or two is the customs office where Jake dropped the cartridge and she hiked up her skirt and we laughed our stoned way through the Mexican criminal-justice system. Off the main drag is the whoring district, a little architectural wonder tossed up to service American soldiers during World War II, and I can see Susan sitting at the small round table in the dark room. She is drinking a rum and Coke, eyeing the women, all a little overweight, their eyes drowning in a lava flow of mascara. Her mouth purses with a small smile. She is dead. She is a corpse.

But I do not say her name. It is not safe. Instead I go to the police station where I see what I expect to see.

The frightened woman propelled by the gunman has long nails painted with red slashes—said to be a gang designation. The Mexican police have rousted her for some questions. She is very silent, the face pockmarked, the eyes unmade. She has been surprised and not given the opportunity to put her best self forward. I wonder how many shoes she owns, what lipsticks lie fallen like soldiers on the top of her dresser. She quickly disappears.

We gather in the office—the windows open to the blast furnace of the street, the magistrate leaning against a wall with a face beaming education, the head cop smiling like broken glass, various flunkies gathered round. The head cop works for the young magistrate but no one sits until the head cop sinks into a folding chair and begins to speak. He allows that El Nacho was "muy famoso." People on the street say he made his first kill at thirteen—an old woman for thirteen cents in change. The cops all have very good, polished shoes—the basic weapon, Colt .45 automatics—and while we speak, a flunky rhythmically stamps a deposition, three stamps to the page. In Nogales, they know of only six kills by El Nacho, four on the street, two in the prison. The head cop continues a litany of petty theft, violence, small scores and quick deaths.

A passing motorist found his body in the tall grass by a road west of Tucson. There were two dead men—hands tied behind their backs, bullets pumped in their heads and torsos. El Nacho was twenty-seven. No one knows much about him—he killed with a knife, or a scissors, or a screwdriver.

I am sitting at another saloon in downtown Nogales, a block

from the fence and the barkeep says, "Oh, yes, El Nacho, he killed my cousin right out front. It was winter and the kids were burning a tire in the street to keep warm, El Nacho, about seventeen, walked up, my cousin Enrique said something, and then El Nacho put a screwdriver through his neck and ran away."

He was a miserable shot and once missed his mistress with a rifle. Some say he killed thirty-eight people—four in Tucson, the rest in Sonora. Some say he killed sixty. He collected debts for others. He believed in the devil but said he doubted God. At his funeral, the woman he lived with came to make sure he was dead—twice before he had been reported killed and yet returned. She looked down at his face, in disbelief—she thought him the devil and how could the devil die?—and she asked the corpse, "What happened to your seven lives?" She carried red roses so as not to appear empty-handed.

We go to the windowless records room where the photos are kept heaped in a shoebox. I look down at his mug shot—a hard face, a black plaque hanging from his neck with white numbers displayed across his chest. He is fifteen years old. He has already killed and within a year will cut down a guard.

They say his brother has just killed a man in Nogales, no? They say his brother found a man speaking unfavorably of El Nacho and for this reason killed. Correct? The cops express no interest.

The rap sheets are typed single spaced—robbery, beatings, gun sales, murder, murder again, and so forth. They hand me his father's sheet and it is long and rich with acts—I meet El Bronco, sire of El Nacho.

A woman with a plain face smiles and hands me a photograph. She says she wishes to attend the University of Arizona and learn English. El Nacho is twenty-five, the expression still hard, the cheekbones more prominent, the eyes gorged and silent with the knowledge there is nothing more to learn with this life. They say he dotted his arm in a spiral—a friend saw the blue swirl of marks in the morgue—and that each dot meant a kill. He told the woman he lived with that the marks meant the devil because Satan has no fixed form. They say his daughter was born with her fingers twisted and curled, the hand flinging the bird at the world.

Upstairs two men are brought in handcuffed. The police put them in a small room with no windows and no air. It is very hot. After a while, the head cop goes in and the two prisoners sit drenched with sweat. The cop feints a blow with one hand, then cracks one guy hard on the chin with the other. He abruptly leaves. As he passes his colleague, busy typing at a desk, he announces, "They're not ready yet."

El Nacho is legend, El Nacho is dead, El Nacho is paper and many stamps and seals. He belongs to me. I lean forward and listen to the Spanish of the police, barely catching the rudest notion of what they are saying. One cop has buxom women in swimsuits under the glass of his desk.

We fondle El Nacho's rap sheets. He is over. And we are not.

Their faces all say they will be with a woman tonight. And renew their belief. And mine.

He is a sociopath, or perhaps a psychopath, a murderer, a crazy, an outlaw. He never belonged in this world and that is why he now only survives in neatly typed rap sheets and tiny mug shots. All attempts to clean him up, to reduce him to reason will fail. They say when he made a kill, he would go home to his barrio and call the police and say, "Come and get me if you can." He supposedly blew away a couple of cops who answered his challenges. The police deny this ever happened. In their records, the past is quite sane and orderly, a few bursts of madness to be sure, but these unpleasant moments are quickly overwhelmed by the logic and good sense of the twentieth century. I look up into the cops' faces and see the seriousness, the dedication, the official facade of the state. Clocks matter, the trains will run on time. El Nacho? The word in the street on Nacho is that his trademark was skinning some of the flesh off his victims. He cannot be made into much of a folk hero until more is forgotten about him. The woman he lived with says he had a very poor sense of time.

But I am here, irresistibly drawn. I can hear Susan laughing again. I can smell the desert seeping through the open windows.

I want a drink, but just one. It will be mezcal. More a toast than a drink.

SOME DEBTS

I read a lot. When I was a boy, I would find my father sitting in the kitchen late at night, smoke curling up from a hand-rolled cigarette, his mind working through a pile of books. The titles would reveal no particular interest, just a jumble of trophies from the adventures of the human race. Maybe this hunger runs in the blood.

This book has sprung from many places, most of which I'll never remember. A few authors were essential: Jack London, Lewis Mumford, H. T. Odum, and William Appleman Williams. And there are the single books that roll around in your mind for months and years: Frederick Turner's *Beyond Geography*, Humphrey Jennings' *Pandaemonium,* Joseph Campbell's *The Hero With a Thousand Faces*, Ken Kesey's *Sometimes a Great Notion,* John Baker's *The Peregrine*, Perry Miller's great biography of Jonathan Edwards.

Also, years ago the John Simon Guggenheim Memorial Foundation gave me a fellowship. After a lot of false steps, dead stick landings, and radical shifts in content, this is the book they helped fund. I want to thank them for their kindness and patience.

No one my age has a sane thought without popular music ringing in their head. But it would be hopeless to explain how thousands of lyrics have formed what I think. Just as it would be a lie to deny it.

ABOUT THE AUTHOR

Author of many acclaimed books about the American Southwest and US-Mexico border issues, CHARLES BOWDEN (1945–2014) was a contributing editor for GQ, *Harper's*, *Esquire*, and *Mother Jones* and also wrote for the *New York Times Book Review*, *High Country News*, and *Aperture*. His honors included a PEN First Amendment Award, Lannan Literary Award for Nonfiction, and the Sidney Hillman Award for outstanding journalism that fosters social and economic justice.